At Issue

Club Drugs

Other Books in the At Issue Series:

At Issue

I Club Drugs

Christine Watkins, Book Editor

GREENHAVEN PRESS
A part of Gale, Cengage Learning

GALE
CENGAGE Learning·

Detroit • New York • San Francisco • New Haven, Conn • Waterville, Maine • London

Elizabeth Des Chenes, *Director, Publishing Solutions*

© 2013 Greenhaven Press, a part of Gale, Cengage Learning.

Gale and Greenhaven Press are registered trademarks used herein under license.

For more information, contact:
Greenhaven Press
27500 Drake Rd.
Farmington Hills, MI 48331-3535
Or you can visit our Internet site at gale.cengage.com

For product information and technology assistance, contact us at

Gale Customer Support, 1-800-877-4253
For permission to use material from this text or product, submit all requests online at
www.cengage.com/permissions

Further permissions questions can be e-mailed to permissionrequest@cengage.com

Articles in Greenhaven Press anthologies are often edited for length to meet page requirements. In addition, original titles of these works are changed to clearly present the main thesis and to explicitly indicate the author's opinion. Every effort is made to ensure that Greenhaven Press accurately reflects the original intent of the authors. Every effort has been made to trace the owners of copyrighted material.

Cover image © Images.com/Corbis.

LIBRARY OF CONGRESS CATALOGING-IN-PUBLICATION DATA

Club drugs / Christine Watkins, book editor.
    p. cm. -- (At issue)
    Includes bibliographical references and index.
    ISBN 978-0-7377-6161-0 (hardcover) -- ISBN 978-0-7377-6162-7 (pbk.)
    1. Ecstasy (Drug) 2. Designer drugs. 3. Designer drugs--Law and legislation. 4. Drug abuse. I. Watkins, Christine, 1951-
    HV5822.M38C587 2013
    362.29'9--dc23
                                                                2012043099

Printed in the United States of America
1 2 3 4 5 6 7 17 16 15 14 13

Contents

Introduction

The term "club drugs" refers to substances commonly used by teens and young adults at dance parties, night clubs, or bars. The drug most readily associated with the term is MDMA, also known as Ecstasy, but other stimulants and hallucinogens are included, such as LSD, GHB, Rohypnol, and amphetamine. The popularity of club drugs stemmed from the rise of the "rave" scene in the late 1970s and early 1980s, when young people gathered in clubs or warehouses with disc jockeys playing electronic dance music, often accompanied by strobe light shows. Known for its energetic and social atmosphere, the rave scene became increasingly popular. Crammed together practically shoulder to shoulder, ravers would dance chaotically for hours to the music's repetitive techno beat. Also during this time, scientists and therapists were studying and prescribing MDMA for its therapeutic benefits, and reports appeared in various medical journals praising the drug's success in marriage therapy and psychoanalysis. It was not long before club-goers heard about MDMA's euphoric effects and began using the drug recreationally to enhance their experience at raves. Simon Reynolds described the drug's attraction to ravers in his book *Energy Flash: A Journey Through Rave Music and Dance Culture*:

> A "psychedelic amphetamine," MDMA is a remarkable chemical, combining the sensory intensification and auditory enhancement of marijuana and low-dose LSD, the sleep-defying, energy boosting effects of speed, and the uninhibited conviviality of alcohol. If that wasn't enough, MDMA offers unique effects of empathy and insights.

Thus MDMA, with its power to create a sense of intimate connection among complete strangers, seemed to fit in perfectly at raves, and it acquired the name Ecstasy. Reynolds explained further, "The blitz of noise and lights at a rave tilts the MDMA experience towards the drug's purely sensuous and sensational effects. With its mildly trippy, pre-hallucinogenic feel, Ecstasy makes colours, sounds, smells, tastes and tactile sensations more vivid."

Because it appeared that Ecstasy was a safe and legal high, its popularity as a club drug soared in the early 1980s. As is often the case, however, too much of a good thing can be ruinous, and this turned out to be true for Ecstasy. Users found that, with sustained and excessive use, the blissful intensity was taken over by feelings of irritability, desolation, and anxiety. Desperate to achieve Ecstasy's original euphoria, users either increased the dosage—which only amplified the unpleasant side effects—or turned to other drugs, such as LSD or amphetamine, or even LSD and amphetamine together. Users experienced increases in body temperature, heart rate, and blood pressure. Some suffered dehydration, muscle cramping, seizures, or paranoia. Inevitably the authorities got involved and in 1985 banned MDMA for one year while they held hearings to determine if it should be categorized on the list of controlled substances as a Schedule 1 drug, the most dangerous and restrictive classification reserved for drugs with a high potential for abuse and no currently accepted medical use. Doctors and scientists challenged the scheduling, but on March 23, 1988, the US Drug Enforcement Administration (DEA) placed MDMA on the Schedule 1 list of illegal drugs.

Teenage and young adult drug consumption continued to thrive, however, despite the fact that most club drugs were banned by the government's Controlled Substances Act. Criminal organizations and drug traffickers took advantage of the underground market and made illicit club drugs easily available. And with the emergence of the Internet, acquiring drugs became even easier. Throughout the 1990s drug abuse ran rampant in the rave scene, and emergency rooms were inundated by overdose patients. Because the drug GHB (gamma hydroxybutyrate, also called liquid ecstasy) affects breathing and the nervous system, many people ended up in comas and some died from its use. Another popular club drug, Rohypnol (flunitrazepam, also called "roofies"), is a central nervous system depressant causing sedative-hypnotic effects, and men began using it as a date-rape drug. In the year 2000 alone, 6.5 million people used Ecstasy, according to the National Institute on Drug Abuse (NIDA).

Today the club drug scene is constantly changing as drug manufacturers alter the psychoactive substances to avoid existing drug laws. These new synthetic drugs—touted as "legal highs" because they are sold as other products, with "Not for Human Consumption" stamped on the packaging—are meant to produce effects similar to their illegal counterparts. For example, drugs marketed as "Spice," incense, or potpourri have been sprayed with chemicals to mimic the effects of marijuana. And users of synthetic amphetamine-type stimulants (ATS) marketed as bath salts and plant food have described the effects as an adrenaline jolt similar to cocaine but with the "warm fuzzies of an Ecstasy trip." The United Nations Office on Drugs and Crime (UNODC) noted in its 2011 *Global ATS Assessment* that an estimated fourteen to fifty-seven million people aged fifteen to sixty-four used an amphetamine-type substance in 2009. This ATS category includes methamphetamine, mephedrone, and Ecstasy. Particularly worrying to authorities are the health risks involved. The NIDA warns, "Uncertainties about the sources, chemicals, and possible contaminants used to manufacture many club drugs make it extremely difficult to determine toxicity and associated medical consequences." Chest pains, increased blood pressure, hallucinations, extreme paranoia, and suicidal thoughts have been reported as side effects. In 2010, Bryan Roudebush attacked his girlfriend and tried to throw her off a Waikiki, Hawaii, balcony while under the influence of "Spice." In 2011, a New Jersey man addicted to bath salts, William Parisio, allegedly beat his girlfriend to death at his home. And in 2012, actress Demi Moore collapsed after reportedly smoking a synthetic incense-like product.

So what should be done, if anything, about the manufacture and use of club drugs? Drug and law enforcement agencies try to monitor the Internet, head shops, convenience stores, and underground labs for the appearance of new drugs, but resources are limited. In her October 29, 2010, *Wall Street Journal* article, Jeanne Whalen explained how David Llewellyn, a "chemically savvy entrepreneur," stays ahead of the law: "He says he's got dozens of other products ready to go. . . . By the time officials crack down, he says, 'we are going to bring out something else.'" In fact, the DEA has temporarily banned some synthetic stimulants while it considers placing them on the scheduled substances list. But other organizations, medical researchers, and scientists believe the government's actions in banning these substances would be problematic. Lee Fadness, a laboratory examiner at the Army Criminal Investigation Laboratory in Georgia told Joe Gould for his October 2, 2010, article in *Army Times*: "You don't want to control everything in the world because some of it has legitimate research use. There's a line between trying to protect people and stopping research completely." The authors of the viewpoints in *At Issue: Club Drugs* discuss these and other perspectives concerning the risks and possible solutions surrounding the use of club drugs.

1

Club Drugs Can Be Harmful

Jim Parker

*Jim Parker is the executive director of the Do It Now Founda-
tion, an organization that creates and distributes accurate and
realistic information on drugs, alcohol, sexuality, and other behavioral health topics.*

*Many people experiment with drugs in order to achieve euphoric
highs—especially people at dance clubs or raves. For example,
some club-goers like to use the drug ecstasy (or MDMA) because
they say it enhances energy and empathy; others prefer ketamine
because it supposedly produces out-of-body experiences; and
2C-B is known to intensify sensory perceptions. But everyone
should keep in mind that these "club" drugs are powerful chemicals that react unpredictably and uniquely in each individual.
Vomiting, dehydration, numbness, slowed heart rate, and even
death are some of the consequences that have resulted from using
these drugs.*

Hey! Maybe the X in Generation X stands for something,
after all. Same for the Y in Generation Y. In fact, maybe
the X stands for X-treme chemical curiosity, and the Y for
"Why not?"

That's one conclusion you could draw, at least, if you felt
the spray off the latest wave of psychoactive chemicals—
including ecstasy, ketamine, GHB, 2C-B, and others—that
crests every night at 11:30 or so in clubs and raves from coast
to coast.

A Reference Guide for Club Drugs

Effects of the drugs span the gamut—ecstasy can inspire speedy feelings of empathy, ketamine out-of-body (and out-of-mind) experiences, GHB a booze-like buzz of bliss and puking, 2C-B giddiness and hallucinations—and they appeal to way different crowds, too.

All-night ravers lean towards ecstasy and, increasingly, the old stimulant standby crystal methamphetamine—which has even lost a few pounds and powdered over some wrinkles for the occasion. New York clubgoers like ketamine, dance-club denizens on the West Coast and elsewhere dig GHB and 2C-B, or "Nexus."

And while users claim all sorts of expanded self-awareness from the drugs, others aren't so sure that satori [enlightenment] can be bought, sold, or borrowed for 20–30 bucks a pop in a nightclub john or a corner of an abandoned warehouse, whether there happens to be a thousand sweaty bodies trance-dancing and pseudo-humping to the thump of 120-beat-a-minute techno music next to you or not.

But, hey, like [comedian and television personality] Dennis Miller used to say (when he was still funny), that's just our opinion. We could be wrong.

The drug that did more than any other to kick off the club-drugs phenomenon is "ecstasy."

A lot of strange stuff has been bubbling up lately in the old club-drugs chemical cauldron. In fact, there are so many new chemicals turning up (and so many pricey, act-alike herbal products masquerading as real drugs) that it's tough telling all the players without a program. Luckily, you've got a program in your hands, right now. In it, we'll be discussing some of the new (and newly-recycled) drugs that are popping up on the dance-club and rave scene.

What we won't be doing is advocating drug use in general or any chemical in particular. We've seen too many lives torn apart in too many ways to endorse the kind of reckless seat-of-the-pants chemistry experiments that people run on themselves.

On the other hand, we know that people will smoke, snort, and swallow just about everything under the sun and moon in pursuing instant enlightenment and nocturnal nirvana, no matter what we say. And we've seen lots of lives wrecked from sheer ignorance, too.

That's why we put together this [information]—because fun really is only one side of the club-drugs risks/benefits equation. The other side is risk, and you need to know as much about that as you can to avoid as much of it as possible.

The Club Drug Ecstasy

The drug that did more than any other to kick off the club-drugs phenomenon is "ecstasy," or MDMA. Chemically related to both methamphetamine and mescaline, it combines properties of both without the excesses of either, according to users. That made it an ideal party drug for lots of people, and it quickly became a staple at "raves," the all-night tribal trance-dances that combine high-energy techno music and the peace-and-love ethic of the new alternative culture.

Users claim that ecstasy (or "E," as it's often called) enhances empathy and catalyzes the rapturous group consciousness that raves are meant to embody, without the perceptual and mental distortions common to such psychedelics as LSD.

On the downside, "E" has been linked to several deaths in the United States and Britain, usually brought on by hyperthermia (high body temperature) and dehydration.

Proponents claim that risks can be minimized by drinking lots of water (or other nonalcoholic liquids) and by taking frequent breaks to avoid overheating during marathon dance sessions.

Ketamine Use as a Club Drug

Ketamine lingered on the fringes of the drug culture for decades, until it was dusted off in the early '90s by Generation X-plorers, impressed by the sheer freakiness of its effects, who turned it into a psychedelic standby in raves and dance clubs.

Used medically as an anesthetic, ketamine differs from other such drugs by stimulating breathing and heart beat, rather than slowing them down. It's also different from other anesthetics (except its chemical cousin, PCP), in its ability to trigger psychological dissociation, hallucinations, even out-of-body experiences and near-death-like states.

The drug [ketamine] can also cause numbness and inco-ordination, even a state of "virtual helplessness."

Still, one person's veggie burger is another person's poison; K's drawbacks as a medical drug serve as its drawing cards as a party drug.

At "subanesthetic" doses (about a tenth of a surgical dose), ketamine triggers major changes in thought and perception, ranging from closed-eye visual hallucinations to "profound transpersonal states," in the words of one researcher. Users undergo a dissolving of normal ego states early in a ketamine experience, accompanied by a sensation of floating or disconnection from the body. Also common are feelings of connection with alternate worlds or parallel dimensions that can seem as real as our own.

The drug can also cause numbness and incoordination, even a state of "virtual helplessness" according to a report in the *British Medical Journal.* And while that may not be a problem if you're home in bed, it can be something else altogether at a rave or dance club.

Finally, using K with alcohol causes vomiting, according to users who presumably learned the usual way.

The Club Drug 2C-B

A relative newcomer on the dance-drug scene, 2C-B produces a variety of effects similar to MDMA. Effects typically start with an "energy tremor," or surge, that occurs during the first 20–30 minutes. Visual distortions and hallucinations are common during the plateau phase of the experience (1-2 hours after ingestion), often accompanied by feelings of insight and heightened emotional awareness and sensitivity. Visual effects associated with 2C-B include intensification of color and transformation of everyday objects or scenes into unusual forms. Other sensory effects include a heightening of smell, touch, and taste, in addition to increased response to color and sound.

> *Symptoms [of GHB] included dizziness, slowed breathing and heart rate, and a "non-rousable" sleep that's sometimes mistaken for coma.*

Although it has no formally-recognized medical uses, 2C-B has been used by a number of therapists, often in conjunction with MDMA. It's also used at raves and in dance clubs, like ecstasy. And just as with ecstasy, liquids should be available during use to reduce the risk of dehydration.

The Drug GHB—Gamma Hydroxybutyrate

If you think ordinary drugs are complex, consider GHB. It's even got two names, GHB (its real name) and GBH—a misabbreviation of an early street name, "Grievous Bodily Harm." Still, all the names and letters refer to the same thing: gamma hydroxybutyrate.

A natural component of normal brain chemistry, GHB was legally available in health stores for years until the U.S. Food and Drug Administration [FDA] banned its sale in 1990, due to adverse reactions linked to its unrestricted use. Early problems were mostly minor, but the FDA launched an investigation that eventually turned up various forms of GHB toxicity. Symptoms included dizziness, slowed breathing and heart rate, and a "non-rousable" sleep that's sometimes mistaken for coma.

As production sloshed onto the black market (via do-it-yourself "chemical kits" sold over the internet), both GHB and a legal chemical precursor, GBL ("Blue Nitro," "Renewtrient"), began to be linked to more problems. The most serious was a potentially life-threatening overdose syndrome, especially when either is used with alcohol. Both were also tied to incidents of drink spiking and date rape—some ending in death—which fueled passage of a nationwide ban in February 2000.

Still, GHB may be as noteworthy for what it symbolizes as for what it is. Because it (and chemicals like it) are bubbling away, even as we speak, in the beakers and brains of Gen-X/Y drug chemists, anxious to put their mark on the hearts and minds of a generation. And the only way we find out whether they succeed or fail is the old-fashioned way: through trial and error, one side effect—or overdose—at a time.

All Drugs Can Be Harmful

To some people, drugs and sex and rock-n-roll go together like, well, like drugs and sex and rock-n-roll. That's been true for a long time. It's no surprise that things aren't different today.

Still, drugs today are different, and they're likely to get even more different in the future. And in spite of any hype you've heard (or may hear) to the contrary, one simple fact about drugs has always been true—and probably always will be. Here it is: [Insert drug name here] is a powerful chemical that can cause serious problems if misused or used under the wrong circumstances. And they can all be misused or used under the wrong circumstances.

It's been true a lot longer than sex and drugs and tribal/trance/techno/hip-hop/trip-hop have gone together: What goes up must come down. And if you want to make sure that the law of cosmic-consciousness cause and effect doesn't come crashing down on you when you least expect it—or are least prepared to deal with it—you'd better remember it.

2

New Synthetic Club Drugs Pose Serious Challenges to Drug Enforcement

Joseph T. Rannazzisi

Joseph T. Rannazzisi is the deputy assistant administrator in the Office of Diversion Control of the Federal Drug Enforcement Administration (DEA).

Marketed as a legal alternative to marijuana, herbal incense products have become increasingly popular, especially among teens and young adults. Herbal incense consists of plant material that has been sprayed with chemicals (synthetic cannabinoids). Likewise, synthetic stimulant compounds that are designed to resemble the effects of cocaine and ecstasy are marketed as bath salts or plant food and are also growing in popularity among drug users. These synthetic compounds have not been approved for human consumption, and there is no regulatory oversight of their manufacturing process. Furthermore, dangerous health effects have been reported from the use of these designer drugs, such as racing heartbeat, seizures, paranoid behavior, and severe psychotic episodes. Controlling the distribution of synthetic drugs is difficult because the Federal Drug Enforcement Administration (DEA) cannot keep up with the endless variations of chemical compounds created by the drug manufacturers.

Joseph T. Rannazzisi, "The Dangers of Synthetic Cannabinoids and Stimulants," Statement for the Record Before the Senate Caucus on International Narcotics Control, United States Senate, April 6, 2011. www.justice.gov/dea.

"Synthetic cannabinoids" are a large family of compounds that are functionally (biologically) similar to THC, the main active ingredient in marijuana. Synthetic cannabinoids, however, are not organic but are chemicals created in a laboratory. . . .

The emergence of synthetic cannabinoids is relatively new to the U.S. "designer drug" market. Since the initial identification of JWH-018 by U.S. forensic laboratories, many additional synthetic cannabinoids including JWH-073, JWH-200, CP-47,497, and cannabicyclohexanol have been identified in related herbal incense products. These synthetic cannabinoids have purported psychotropic effects when smoked or ingested. These chemicals are typically found in powder form or are dissolved in solvents, such as acetone, before being sprayed on the plant material comprising the "herbal incense" products.

> *The packaging is professional and conspicuous and targets young people, possibly eager to use cannabis, but who are afraid of the legal consequences and/or association with illicit drugs.*

Synthetic Cannabinoids Are Marketed as Legal Marijuana

The popularity of these THC-like synthetic cannabinoids has significantly increased throughout the United States, and they are being abused for their psychoactive properties as reported by law enforcement agencies, the medical community, and in scientific literature. They are marketed as a "legal" alternative to marijuana or other drugs. They are also popular among those individuals who are subject to urinalysis testing, such as those individuals who are under the supervision of a drug court and those on probation or parole.

Some of the product names include, but are not limited to, "Spice," "K2," "Zohai," "Dream," "Genie," "Sence," "Smoke,"

"Skunk," "Serenity," "Yucatan," "Fire," and many more. These products are labeled "Not for Human Consumption" and are typically advertised as herbal incense by Internet retailers, tobacco shops, head shops, and other domestic brick and mortar retail venues. These marketing techniques result in the perception that products that contain THC-like synthetic cannabinoids are "legal" alternatives to marijuana. No evidence exists that these synthetic cannabinoids add value to genuine incense products—there is no scent or odor associated with these substances.

According to Internet discussion boards and law enforcement encounters reported directly to DEA [Drug Enforcement Administration], synthetic cannabinoids are sprayed on plant material which provides a vehicle for the most common route of administration—smoking (using a pipe, a water pipe, or rolling the drug-spiked plant material in cigarette papers). These materials were then packaged in small pouches or packets sold over the Internet, in tobacco and smoke shops, drug paraphernalia shops, gas stations, and convenience stores as herbal incense products. The retail sale of these products gave customers of all ages direct access to synthetic cannabinoids and the corresponding THC-like effects of these products. Research articles propose that the packaging is professional and conspicuous and targets young people, possibly eager to use cannabis, but who are afraid of the legal consequences and/or association with illicit drugs. . . .

Case reports describe psychotic episodes, withdrawal, and dependence associated with use of these synthetic cannabinoids.

On March 24, 2010, the American Association of Poison Control Centers reported that, since 2009, there were 112 calls to U.S. poison control centers from 15 different states related to synthetic cannabinoids. Just nine months later, the number increased to over 2,700 calls from 49 different states and the District of Columbia.

Risk to the Public Health

Health warnings have been issued by numerous state and local public health departments and poison control centers describing the adverse health effects associated with the use of these synthetic cannabinoids and their related products, including agitation, anxiety, nausea, vomiting, tachycardia (fast, racing heartbeat), elevated blood pressure, tremor, seizures, hallucinations, paranoid behavior, and non-responsiveness.

Smoking synthetic cannabinoids for the purpose of achieving intoxication and experiencing the psychoactive effects has been identified as a reason for emergency room visits and calls to poison control centers. In a fact sheet issued by the National Drug Court Institute, the problem of synthetic cannabinoid abuse is described as "significant and disturbing." This is supported by information that was communicated to DEA from one of the major private toxicology laboratories. Specifically, laboratory findings from drug screens for the period July 2010 through November 2010 showed over 3,700 specimens tested positive for either JWH-018 or JWH-073. They also indicated that they were finding 30–35% positivity for specimens submitted by juvenile probation departments.

Case reports describe psychotic episodes, withdrawal, and dependence associated with use of these synthetic cannabinoids, similar to syndromes observed in marijuana abuse. Based on law enforcement encounters reported directly to DEA, when responding to incidents involving individuals who have reportedly smoked these synthetic cannabinoids, first responders report that these individuals have suffered from intense hallucinations. Emergency department physicians and toxicologists have also reported the adverse health effects associated with smoking herbal incense products laced with these substances. Law enforcement agencies have recently reported examples of suspected *Driving under the Influence of Drug* incidents that were attributed to the smoking of synthetic cannabinoids. For example, in September 2010, police in Nebraska responded to an incident involving a teenager who had careened his truck into the side of a residence. After striking the residence and several more items, the teen continued several more yards before coming to a complete stop. Prior to crashing the truck, the individual had driven past a junior high school and nearly struck a child. Upon further investigation, the driver of the vehicle admitted to smoking "Wicked X," a product marketed as "herbal incense" and known to contain synthetic cannabinoids, prior to the accident. Preliminary toxicology reports indicated that the individual did not have any alcohol or other illegal substances in his system.

The herbal incense products are manufactured in the absence of quality controls and devoid of governmental regulatory oversight.

Detailed chemical analyses by DEA and other agencies have found these synthetic cannabinoids spiked on plant material in herbal incense products marketed to the general public. Product analyses have found variations in both the type of synthetic cannabinoid and the amount of the substance found on the plant material. As proposed in scientific literature, the risk of adverse health effects is further increased by the fact that similar products vary in the composition and concentration of synthetic cannabinoids spiked on the plant material.

Self-reported abuse of these THC-like synthetic cannabinoids either alone (*e.g.*, in pills or with the substance in powder form) or spiked on plant material appear extensively on Internet discussion boards, and abuse has been reported to public health officials and law enforcement agencies. The abuse of these substances in the smoked form (sprayed on plant material) has been corroborated by forensic laboratory analysis of products encountered by law enforcement agencies.

Staying One Step Ahead of Government Oversight

According to U.S. Customs and Border Protection, a number of the products and synthetic cannabinoids appear to originate from foreign sources. Product manufacturing operations encountered by law enforcement personnel establish that the herbal incense products are manufactured in the absence of quality controls and devoid of governmental regulatory oversight. Law enforcement personnel have encountered the manufacture of herbal incense products in such places as residential neighborhoods. These products and associated synthetic cannabinoids are readily accessible via the Internet.

Even though several of these compounds have been controlled/banned in some states, and temporarily scheduled by DEA, scientists are able to continue to provide retailers with "legal" products by developing/synthesizing new synthetic cannabinoid products that are not covered under state/ Federal regulatory, administrative or statutory actions. Retail entrepreneurs are able to procure new synthetic cannabinoid products, which have comparative psychoactive properties, with relative ease. In fact, after DEA took action to temporarily schedule [as a controlled substance] the five (5) initial cannabinoid products, retailers began selling new versions of the products that did not contain the banned cannabinoids, but instead new version JWH compounds. The retailers were provided with a chemical analysis that documented that the new product line did not contain any of the banned cannabinoids.

In Kansas, a major manufacturer/distributor of synthetic cannabinoid products told a law enforcement officer, ". . . if the compound that he is using, JWH-250, is banned, he would just switch and treat his dried plant material with another legal compound." There may be in excess of 100 cannabinoid products that have yet to be introduced into the marketplace. Manufacturers and distributors will continue to stay one step ahead of any state or Federal drug-specific banning or control action by introducing/repackaging new cannabinoid products that are not controlled. . . .

> *They are indirectly marketed as "legal" alternatives to the controlled substances cocaine, amphetamine, [and] Ecstasy.*

It is clear that the income generated from distributing these products is, and will continue to be, a driving factor for retailers to seek/find substitute products that are not yet controlled or banned by Federal or state action. This is reminiscent of the typical illicit drug dealer cost-benefit analysis, in which the potential for financial gain far outweighs the potential for legal consequences. The large profits and the fact that these chemicals can be easily synthesized to stay one step ahead of control, indicate there is no incentive to discontinue retail distribution of synthetic cannabinoid products under the current statutory and regulatory scheme. Although many good corporate citizen retailers will discontinue the sale of these products in support of public health and safety, many will not, instead opting for the profits realized to help their financial "bottom line".

Dangerous Synthetic Drugs Sold as Legal Stimulants

Another serious drug threat that has recently emerged is the growing distribution and abuse of a class of synthetic substances that have stimulant/psychoactive properties when ingested and that are sold as "bath salts" or "plant food." On February 1, 2011, director of national Drug Control Policy Gil Kerlikowske issued a press release concerning the emerging threat of synthetic stimulants. In his statement, Director Kerlikowske stated, "I am deeply concerned about the distribution, sale and use of synthetic stimulants—especially those that are marketed as legal substances. Although we lack sufficient data to understand exactly how prevalent the use of these stimulants is, we know they pose a serious threat to the health and well being of young people and anyone who may use them."

These products are sold under a variety of brand names including "Ivory Wave," "Vanilla Sky," "Energy-1" (NRG-1), "Ocean Snow," "Hurricane Charlie," "White Lightening," "Red Dove," "Cloud-9," "White Dove," "White Girl" and many others. They are indirectly marketed as "legal" alternatives to the controlled substances cocaine, amphetamine, Ecstasy (MDMA or 3,4-methylenedioxymethamphetamine) and methcathinone. The most prevalent synthetic substances encountered within these products include MDPV (3,4-methylenedioxy pyrovalerone), mephedrone (4-methylmethcathinone) and methylone (3,4-methylenedioxymethcathinone). These drugs have been distributed and abused in Europe, particularly Great Britain and Germany, for several years. Mephedrone was first detected as a drug of abuse in Europe in November 2007.

These synthetic substances are suspected to be manufactured in bulk quantities in countries such as China, Pakistan, and India, and some of the actual products may be packaged for wholesale distribution in intermediate locations such as Eastern Europe.

The appearance of these designer drugs in products being sold in the United States has proliferated because of the Internet. These substances are marketed as "research chemicals," "plant food," or "bath salts," not for human consumption, to circumvent the CSA [Controlled Substances Act]. Products are sold in a powder form that can be easily ingested. Marketing in this manner attempts to hide the true reason for the products' existence—the distribution of a psychoactive/

stimulant substance for abuse. As with the synthetic cannabinoids, these synthetic stimulants are sold at smoke shops, head shops, convenience stores, adult book stores, and gas stations, in addition to over the Internet. Retailers that sell these products post a disclaimer on their websites that their products are "not intended for human consumption," in an attempt to circumvent statutory and regulatory controls. Websites often list products containing these synthetic stimulants as "plant food;" however, the powdered form is encapsulated in gelatin capsules, and dealers offer "discreet delivery" to the potential customer. Additionally, these products retail at prices that are considerably higher than legitimately marketed plant food or bath salt products. They are even known on the street by nicknames such as "Meow Meow," "drone," or "Molly".

A number of states, including Florida, Louisiana, North Dakota, and West Virginia, have imposed emergency measures to ban retail products, such as bath salts, that contain synthetic stimulant substances; and similar measures are pending in Hawaii, Kentucky, Michigan, and Mississippi. Additionally, the trend in the development, distribution, and consumption of this class of substances in Europe has resulted in the United Kingdom and Germany banning products containing these substances. . . .

What is known about these chemicals is disconcerting. There have been reports in the media of overdoses from ingestion of "bath salt" products which resulted in emergency room visits, hospitalizations, and severe psychotic episodes, some of which have led to violent outbursts, self-inflicted wounds, and, in at least one instance, suicide. Abusers of "bath salt" products have reported that they experienced many adverse effects such as chest pain, increased blood pressure, increased heart rate, agitation, panic attacks, hallucinations, extreme paranoia, and delusions.

Some users have reported anecdotally that they have "crashed" or "comedown" from mephedrone with effects similar to those they experienced from "coming down" from ecstasy and cocaine. Users of "bath salt" products self-administer the drugs by snorting the powder, smoking it, or injecting themselves intravenously....

They can create substances that are pharmacologically similar to a schedule I or II controlled substance.

The Challenge of Newly Created Synthetic Compounds

The DEA Administrator published a final order on March 1, 2011, placing five synthetic cannabinoids into the CSA pursuant to the temporary scheduling provisions of the CSA. During the temporary scheduling period, DEA will continue to gather and analyze scientific data and other information collected from all sources, including poison control centers, hospitals, and law enforcement agencies, in order to demonstrate that these substances should be permanently scheduled....

Controlling the distribution and abuse of newly synthesized analogues [chemical compounds derived from another compound] is challenging because, as DEA investigates, researches, and develops evidence pertinent to potential analogue substances in support of administrative control, illicit drug makers abandon these substances and create *new* analogue substances. Such a circular pursuit requires the expenditure of substantial scientific and investigative resources and continually leaves government scientists, regulators, and investigators one step behind the traffickers....

The challenge to controlling these substances individually through administrative actions pursuant to the CSA is that the manufacturers of these substances circumvent the statutory criteria by manipulating the chemical structure of the compound. They can create substances that are pharmacologically similar to a schedule I or II controlled substance, that may or may not be chemically (structurally) similar to a schedule I or II controlled substance. The statute requires both pharmacological and chemical similarity in order to be an analogue. Even more alarming is that the structure of a chemical substance can be manipulated in *endless variations* while the pharmacological activity of the substance may increase or remain substantially unchanged. As a result, it is almost impossible outside of a controlled laboratory environment to determine the chemical composition, and the quantity, potency, and type of synthetic ingredients in these substances. It is equally challenging to determine what the potential harmful effects may be due to human consumption. . . .

In closing, DEA will continue to work with its local, state and federal counterparts to protect the public against the dangers of these ever-changing synthetic cannabinoids, stimulant compounds and "designer" drugs.

3

Legislation Is Needed to Ban Synthetic Club Drugs

Charles E. Grassley

Charles E. Grassley, a member of the Republican Party, is the senior US senator from Iowa and the co-chairman of the Caucus on International Narcotics Control.

More and more young people today—including members of the military—are buying and using drugs that are innocently marketed as "incense," "spice," or "bath salts," but which are, in fact, sprayed with powerful and dangerous chemicals. The use of these new synthetic drugs can cause serious health effects, such as hallucinations, paranoia, and racing heart beat; users have also been known to harm other people and even kill themselves. Because these synthetic drugs can be easily purchased in stores or online, legislation is necessary to ban the chemical compounds associated with the products so they can be removed from the market.

Drugs disguised and marketed as harmless products such as incense, bath salts or even plant food are rapidly gaining in popularity among America's youth. These products are combined with powerful and potent synthetic drugs and stimulants that reportedly mimic the effects of other dangerous and illegal drugs. These drugs have been sold in mainstream convenience stores, shopping malls, gas stations, and on several internet websites. Popular brand names for these

Charles E. Grassley, "The Dangers of Synthetic Cannabinoids and Stimulants," Opening Statement, Senate Caucus on International Narcotics Control, April 6, 2011.

products include: "K2," "Spice," "Ivory Wave," "Red Dove," and "Vanilla Sky" among many others. According to several news reports, many people who use these products often cite the fact that they can get these products easily by going to the nearest store or simply purchasing them online. The ease with which these products are available and the fact that they are not completely banned in this country may lead users to believe that using these products is nothing more than harmless fun. It is now clear that using these products is anything but harmless.

Synthetic Drugs Cause Serious Health Effects

According to a statement from Dr. Anthony Scalzo, who is the Medical Director of the Missouri Poison Center and Director of Toxicology at Saint Louis University, these products cause serious health effects including symptoms such as: racing heart beat, elevated blood pressure, hallucinations, anxiety, agitation and significant delusions and paranoia. Dr. Scalzo also describes cases where patients have become dependent on these drugs and where users have seriously harmed themselves, committed crimes, and harmed others while high on these substances.

Police arrested a 23-year-old man after he tried to throw his girlfriend off an 11th floor balcony after smoking K2.

Dr. Scalzo also adds that U.S. poison control centers are reporting skyrocketing calls regarding these drugs. According to Dr. Scalzo's statement, poison centers reported over 2,800 calls concerning synthetic marijuana known as "K2" or "Spice." As of March 22nd [2011], there have already been over 1,200 calls to poison control centers concerning synthetic marijuana products this year alone. That means we're on pace to have over 4,800 calls for 2011, which would be nearly a 60% increase. Further, poison control centers have taken over 1,200 calls so far this year concerning "bath salts" use. This is more than a 400% increase from all calls received concerning "bath salts" in 2010. These numbers don't paint the whole picture of the extent of the use of these products, but they do illustrate that more people are using these products and experiencing serious effects. . . .

The armed forces are also experiencing increasing cases of synthetic drug use. It was with sadness and concern that I recently read about K2 being used by members in the armed services and at the service academies. According to a recent article in the *Navy Times*, 16 sailors serving on the *U.S.S. Bataan* were recently discharged for using "Spice." The U.S.S. Bataan has since been deployed to Libya short these sailors. The article further states that 151 sailors Navy-wide had been accused of using or caught with "Spice" over the last four months. The U.S. Naval Academy also recently expelled at least 7 midshipmen for using or selling "Spice." The use of these drugs among our men and women serving in the armed forces is especially concerning from an operational and readiness standpoint while our armed services are still engaged in Afghanistan, Iraq, and beginning operations in Libya.

According to various news articles across the nation, synthetic drug use can cause serious erratic and criminal behavior. In Mooresville, Indiana, police arrested a group of teens after they were connected to a string of burglaries while high on K2. Another case in Honolulu, Hawaii, shows police arrested a 23-year-old man after he tried to throw his girlfriend off an 11th floor balcony after smoking K2. A 14-year-old boy in Missouri nearly threw himself out of a 5th story window after smoking K2. Once the teen got over his high he denied having any suicidal intentions. Doctors believe he was hallucinating at the time of this incident.

Death Can Result from Synthetic Drug Use

Synthetic drug use also has deadly consequences. This past June [2010] a young constituent of mine, named David Rozga . . . , was a recent graduate of Indianola High School in Indianola, Iowa. David committed suicide shortly after smoking a packet of "K2." David and his friends purchased "K2" at an area shopping mall thinking it could not have been dangerous if you could get it at the mall. . . . David Rozga may have been the first person in the U.S. to have died from using these products, but tragically he has not been the last.

News articles from across the country are reporting deaths as a result of synthetic drug use. A month after David's tragic death police report that a 28-year-old Middletown, Indiana, mother of two passed away after smoking a lethal dose of K2. This woman's godson reported that anyone could get K2 easily because it can be sold to anybody at any price at any time. This last August, a recent 19-year-old Lake Highlands High School graduate in Dallas, Texas, passed away after smoking K2. The medical examiner confirmed that this boy had K2 in his system at the time of his death. A man in Louisiana slit his throat and shot himself while hallucinating on "bath salts" last year. Another case in Louisiana occurred last year when a 21-year-old man suffered for three days after smoking "bath salts." This man slit his throat while hallucinating. Although he missed major arteries he was still under the influence of the drug. When his dad, who was a medical doctor and treating him, fell asleep, his son went into another room and shot himself. Even more disturbing is the involvement of synthetic drugs in a recent school shooting that occurred in Omaha, Nebraska, last January. Robert Butler Jr. shot and killed himself and Dr. Vicki Kaspar, the assistant principal at the school. Doctors have confirmed that Robert Butler had K2 in his system at the time of the shooting.

Legislation Is Needed to Ban Synthetic Drugs

These incidents I've described only scratch the surface of the growing abuse and tragedy synthetic drugs are having on this nation. All of us on this panel [Senate Caucus on International Narcotics Control] are deeply concerned about the continued availability of these drugs. Chairman [Dianne] Feinstein and I recently introduced legislation, named after David Rozga, to ban the chemical compounds the DEA [Drug Enforcement Administration] has identified within K2/Spice products. The legislation will also amend the Controlled Substances Act, doubling the timeframe the DEA and the Department of Health and Human Services have to emergency schedule substances from 18 months to 36 months. This will allow for dangerous substances to be quickly removed from the market while being studied for permanent scheduling. Senator [Charles E.] Schumer and Representative [Charles] Dent of Pennsylvania have also introduced legislation to schedule synthetic drugs like "bath salts" and other products.

Madam Chairman, you and I have worked closely together on many issues especially when it comes to illegal drugs. I really appreciate your efforts in joining me to ensure these dangerous drugs are removed from our society.

4

Club Drugs Can Be Used to Facilitate Rape

Office on Women's Health

A project of the US Department of Health and Human Services, the Office on Women's Health works to improve the health and sense of well-being of all US women and girls through innovative programs and local public health initiatives.

Rohypnol, GHB, ketamine, and ecstasy are known as "club drugs" because they tend to be used at dance clubs and raves. Taking these drugs can be risky, however, because the resulting physical reactions—such as loss of muscle control, dizziness, and loss of memory while drugged—can make the individual an easy target for rape. Making matters worse, the drugs often have no color or taste, so they can be added to a drink without a person's knowledge. To protect themselves from sexual assault, people need to be aware of the risks involved with club drugs and should be extremely vigilant at all times.

[D]ate rape drugs] are drugs that are sometimes used to assist a sexual assault. Sexual assault is any type of sexual activity that a person does not agree to. It can include touching that is not okay, putting something into the vagina, sexual intercourse, rape, and attempted rape. These drugs are powerful and dangerous. They can be slipped into your drink when you are not looking. The drugs often have no color, smell, or taste, so you can't tell if you are being drugged. The

Office on Women's Health (OWH), "Date Rape Drugs Fact Sheet," WomensHealth.gov, last updated December 5, 2008. www.womenshealth.gov/publications/our-publications/fact-sheet/date-rape-drugs.cfm.

drugs can make you become weak and confused—or even pass out—so that you are unable to refuse sex or defend yourself. If you are drugged, you might not remember what happened while you were drugged. Date rape drugs are used on both females and males.

Alcohol makes the drugs even stronger and can cause serious health problems—even death.

The three most common date rape drugs are:

- *Rohypnol* (roh-HIP-nol). Rohypnol is the trade name for flunitrazepam (FLOO-neye-TRAZ-uh-pam). Abuse of two similar drugs appears to have replaced Rohypnol abuse in some parts of the United States. These are: clonazepam (marketed as Klonopin in the U.S. and Rivotril in Mexico) and alprazolam (marketed as Xanax). Rohypnol is also known as: Circles, Forget Pill, LA Rochas, Lunch Money, Mexican Valium, Mind Erasers, Poor Man's Quaalude, R-2, Rib, Roach, Roach-2, Roches, Roofies, Roopies, Rope, Rophies, Ruffies, Trip-and-Fall, [and] Whiteys.

- *GHB*, which is short for gamma hydroxybutyric (GAM-muh heye-DROX-ee-BYOO-tur-ihk) acid. GHB is also known as: Bedtime Scoop, Cherry Meth, Easy Lay, Energy Drink, G, Gamma 10, Georgia Home Boy, G-Juice, Gook, Goop, Great Hormones, Grievous Bodily Harm (GBH), Liquid E, Liquid Ecstasy, Liquid X, PM, Salt Water, Soap, Somatomax, [and] Vita-G.

- *Ketamine* (KEET-uh-meen), also known as: Black Hole, Bump, Cat Valium, Green, Jet, K, K-Hole, Kit Kat, Psychedelic Heroin, Purple, Special K, [and] Super Acid.

These drugs also are known as "club drugs" because they tend to be used at dance clubs, concerts, and "raves."

The term "date rape" is widely used. But most experts prefer the term "drug-facilitated sexual assault." These drugs also are used to help people commit other crimes, like robbery and physical assault. They are used on both men and women. The term "date rape" also can be misleading because the person who commits the crime might not be dating the victim. Rather, it could be an acquaintance or stranger.

What Do the Drugs Look Like?

- Rohypnol comes as a pill that dissolves in liquids. Some are small, round, and white. Newer pills are oval and green-gray in color. When slipped into a drink, a dye in these new pills makes clear liquids turn bright blue and dark drinks turn cloudy. But this color change might be hard to see in a dark drink, like cola or dark beer, or in a dark room. Also, the pills with no dye are still available. The pills may be ground up into a powder.

- GHB has a few forms: a liquid with no odor or color, white powder, and pill. It might give your drink a slightly salty taste. Mixing it with a sweet drink, such as fruit juice, can mask the salty taste.

- Ketamine comes as a liquid and a white powder.

Ketamine is very fast-acting. You might be aware of what is happening to you, but unable to move.

What Effects Do These Drugs Have on the Body?

These drugs are very powerful. They can affect you very quickly and without your knowing. The length of time that the effects last varies. It depends on how much of the drug is taken and if the drug is mixed with other drugs or alcohol. Alcohol makes the drugs even stronger and can cause serious health problems—even death.

The effects of Rohypnol can be felt within 30 minutes of being drugged and can last for several hours. If you are drugged, you might look and act like someone who is drunk. You might have trouble standing. Your speech might be slurred. Or you might pass out. Rohypnol can cause these problems: muscle relaxation or loss of muscle control, difficulty with motor movements, drunk feeling, problems talking, nausea, can't remember what happened while drugged, loss of consciousness (black out), confusion, problems seeing, dizziness, sleepiness, lower blood pressure, stomach problems, [and] death.

GHB takes effect in about 15 minutes and can last 3 or 4 hours. It is very potent. A very small amount can have a big effect. So it's easy to overdose on GHB. Most GHB is made by people in home or street "labs," so you don't know what's in it or how it will affect you. GHB can cause these problems: relaxation, drowsiness, dizziness, nausea, problems seeing, loss of consciousness (black out), seizures, can't remember what happened while drugged, problems breathing, tremors, sweating, vomiting, slow heart rate, dream-like feeling, coma, [and] death.

Ketamine is very fast-acting. You might be aware of what is happening to you, but unable to move. It also causes memory problems. Later, you might not be able to remember what happened while you were drugged. Ketamine can cause these problems: distorted perceptions of sight and sound, lost sense of time and identity, out of body experiences, dream-like feeling, feeling out of control, impaired motor function, problems breathing, convulsions, vomiting, memory problems, numbness, loss of coordination, aggressive or violent behavior, depression, high blood pressure, [and] slurred speech.

Are These Drugs Legal in the United States?

Some of these drugs are legal when lawfully used for medical purposes. But that doesn't mean they are safe. These drugs are powerful and can hurt you. They should only be used under a doctor's care and order.

- Rohypnol is not legal in the United States. It is legal in Europe and Mexico, where it is prescribed for sleep problems and to assist anesthesia before surgery. It is brought into the United States illegally.

- Ketamine is legal in the United States for use as an anesthetic for humans and animals. It is mostly used on animals. Veterinary clinics are robbed for their ketamine supplies.

- GHB was recently made legal in the United States to treat problems from narcolepsy (a sleep disorder). Distribution of GHB for this purpose is tightly restricted.

What About Other Drugs?

Any drug that can affect judgment and behavior can put a person at risk for unwanted or risky sexual activity. Alcohol is one such drug. In fact, alcohol is the drug most commonly used to help commit sexual assault. When a person drinks too much alcohol:

- It's harder to think clearly.

- It's harder to set limits and make good choices.

- It's harder to tell when a situation could be dangerous.

- It's harder to say "no" to sexual advances.

- It's harder to fight back if a sexual assault occurs.

- It's possible to blackout and to have memory loss.

The club drug "ecstasy" (MDMA) has been used to commit sexual assault. It can be slipped into someone's drink without the person's knowledge. Also, a person who willingly takes ecstasy is at greater risk of sexual assault. Ecstasy can make a person feel "lovey-dovey" towards others. It also can lower a person's ability to give reasoned consent. Once under the drug's influence, a person is less able to sense danger or to resist a sexual assault.

Most victims don't remember being drugged or assaulted.

Even if a victim of sexual assault drank alcohol or willingly took drugs, the victim is *not* at fault for being assaulted. You cannot "ask for it" or cause it to happen.

How Can I Protect Myself from Being a Victim?

- Don't accept drinks from other people.

- Open containers yourself.

- Keep your drink with you at all times, even when you go to the bathroom.

- Don't share drinks.

- Don't drink from punch bowls or other common, open containers. They may already have drugs in them.

- If someone offers to get you a drink from a bar or at a party, go with the person to order your drink. Watch the drink being poured and carry it yourself.

- Don't drink anything that tastes or smells strange. Sometimes, GHB tastes salty.

- Have a nondrinking friend with you to make sure

nothing happens.

- If you realize you left your drink unattended, pour it out.

- If you feel drunk and haven't drunk any alcohol—or, if you feel like the effects of drinking alcohol are stronger than usual—get help right away.

Are There Ways to Tell If I Might Have Been Drugged and Raped?

It is often hard to tell. Most victims don't remember being drugged or assaulted. The victim might not be aware of the attack until 8 or 12 hours after it occurred. These drugs also leave the body very quickly. Once a victim gets help, there might be no proof that drugs were involved in the attack. But there are some signs that you might have been drugged:

- You feel drunk and haven't drunk any alcohol—or, you feel like the effects of drinking alcohol are stronger than usual.

- You wake up feeling very hung over and disoriented or having no memory of a period of time.

- You remember having a drink, but cannot recall anything after that.

- You find that your clothes are torn or not on right.

- You feel like you had sex, but you cannot remember it.

What Should I Do If I Think I've Been Drugged and Raped?

- Get medical care right away. Call 911 or have a trusted friend take you to a hospital emergency room. Don't urinate, douche, bathe, brush your teeth, wash your hands, change clothes, or eat or drink before you go.

These things may give evidence of the rape. The hospital will use a "rape kit" to collect evidence.

- Call the police from the hospital. Tell the police exactly what you remember. Be honest about all your activities. Remember, nothing you did—including drinking alcohol or doing drugs—can justify rape.

- Ask the hospital to take a urine (pee) sample that can be used to test for date rape drugs. The drugs leave your system quickly. Rohypnol stays in the body for several hours, and can be detected in the urine up to 72 hours after taking it. GHB leaves the body in 12 hours. Don't urinate before going to the hospital.

- Don't pick up or clean up where you think the assault might have occurred. There could be evidence left behind—such as on a drinking glass or bed sheets.

- Get counseling and treatment. Feelings of shame, guilt, fear, and shock are normal. A counselor can help you work through these emotions and begin the healing process. Calling a crisis center or a hotline is a good place to start. One national hotline is the *National Sexual Assault Hotline at 800-656-HOPE.*

5

Ecstasy Use by Pregnant Women Can Affect Infant Development

Case Western Reserve University School of Medicine

Case Western Reserve University School of Medicine is the largest medical research institution in Ohio.

Because the use of ecstasy is widespread throughout the world, many child development experts and medical researchers are concerned that pregnant women may also be using ecstasy, thereby exposing their unborn babies to adverse health risks. A new study is underway to compare infants exposed to ecstasy with those not exposed. Data will be collected for babies up to eighteen months old. Early results from the study suggest that ecstasy does indeed affect the motor functioning of infants and also contributes to developmental delays.

Ecstasy is a stimulant and hallucinogen, and is one of the most widely used illegal drugs among young people, with a range of damaging effects. It is known scientifically as 3,4-methylenedioxymethamphetamine or MDMA. This international prospective study, published in the Feb. 28 [2012] issue of *Neurotoxicology and Teratology*, shows that use of ecstasy among pregnant women affects the chemical signaling that determines a baby's gender and contributes to developmental delays among infants.

Concern About Prenatal Exposure to Ecstacy Prompts Study

"The potential harmful effects of ecstasy exposure on prenatal and infant development have long been a concern," said Lynn T. Singer, PhD, the study's principal investigator, professor of environmental health sciences, pediatrics and psychiatry at Case Western Reserve University School of Medicine and deputy provost and vice president for academic affairs at the university. "The drug's negative effects are particularly risky for pregnant women, who may use the drug without being aware of their condition," she adds.

The study's 96 participants were recruited from the University of East London (UEL) Drugs and Infancy Study (DAISY), which focused on recreational drug use among pregnant women. Prior to and during pregnancy, the women were interviewed about their substance abuse, including their use of ecstasy. They were also evaluated for psychiatric symptoms and related difficulties that stemmed from their drug use.

Researchers compared infants exposed to ecstasy to non-exposed infants, at birth and at fourth months of age. They examined the babies' growth and noted any potential delays in cognitive development and attainment of milestones in coordinated movements and gross motor development.

Ecstasy-exposed infants in the study demonstrated poorer quality of coordinated movement and lower milestone attainment.

Most of the women surveyed had taken a variety of illegal drugs prior to and during pregnancy. Differences among the women were analyzed to control for confounding variables. Researchers found that women who reported using ecstasy while pregnant suffered more negative social consequences as a result of their ecstasy use than non-users. These included more job, health and social problems.

The use of ecstasy during pregnancy also appeared to affect the ratio of male to female babies born. Researchers noted a preponderance of male births among women who used ecstasy while pregnant, whereas typically the sex ratio at birth is half and half.

"The research findings also suggests there are some neurochemical effects of the drug that seem to affect the motor functioning of infants," says Derek Moore, PhD, professor of psychology at the University of East London, director of the school's Institute for Research in Child Development (IRCD) and co-principal investigator on this research. He coordinated the research in the UK [United Kingdom].

Early Research Results Show Possible Brain Alteration

At four months, ecstasy-exposed infants in the study demonstrated poorer quality of coordinated movement and lower milestone attainment, according to Dr. Moore. For example, some ecstasy-exposed infants balanced their heads at a later age than babies that were not exposed to the drug. Others showed delays in eye hand coordination, turning from back to side and being able to sit with support, which could heighten the potential for additional developmental delays later on.

If the level and behavior of serotonin is altered, it can have long-term effects on learning and memory.

The research underscores a potential link between the amounts of ecstasy exposure to poorer motor quality, which warrants further study, Dr. Singer says.

Ecstasy is such a widely used drug throughout the world, that if prenatal exposure is shown to be harmful, many infants could be affected, the researchers say.

"The psychomotor and related psychological problems identified in these four-month-old babies are very worrying, but perhaps not particularly surprising," says Andy Parrott, BSc, PhD, professor of psychology at Swansea University in Wales and the other co-principal investigator on this research. "Ecstasy can deplete the level of serotonin, which is [an] important neurotransmitter for many brain functions, including gross motor control."

Serotonin carries nerve impulses between cells, which regulate mood states, sleep and anxiety. Early in fetal development, serotonin plays a vital role in brain formation. If the level and behavior of serotonin is altered, it can have long-term effects on learning and memory, basic research models have shown.

The new research grew out of Dr. Singer's ongoing research into high-risk infants and the effects that drugs have on fetal and infant development. She became familiar with the work of Dr. Parrott at Swansea and Dr. Moore and John Turner, PhD, principal lecturer in the School of Psychology at the University of East London, and initiated this important prospective study to investigate the prospective effects of ecstasy on subsequent child development.

The study was funded by the National Institute on Drug Abuse, part of the National Institutes of Health. It is funded to collect data up to 18 months after an infant's birth. Researchers are examining the same women and children 12 months after birth to assess if the slight delays noted early on worsen or persist, potentially signaling the long-term negative effect of prenatal ecstasy exposure.

The researchers hope to obtain additional funding to continue the study well into the infants' childhood years. The fear [is] that, in the future, the infants exposed to ecstasy prior to birth may experience long-term deficits that will negatively affect their memory, learning capacity, and emotional development.

6

Recreational Use of the Club Drug Ketamine Can Lead to Bladder Disease

Dina Rickman

Dina Rickman is a journalist and the assistant politics editor at The Huffington Post *in the United Kingdom.*

The current club drug of choice among young people in the United Kingdom is ketamine, with an estimated 125,000 users. But as its popularity rises, the number of people reporting serious side effects from the drug is rising along with it. For example, severe stomach pains—known as "k cramps"—are associated with ketamine use, as well as blood in the urine, incontinence, and painful urination. In some cases, bladders needed to be surgically removed because the drug caused so much damage.

Three teenagers are huddled over a CD case in the corner of a Brighton [England] squat. Rave music blares from the soundsystem as they cut lines of white powder from a crumpled wrap. Emily, the youngest of the group at 17, uses a £5 note to snort the largest line. She laughs, coughs a little, then passes the CD case to her friend. "This is just like Skins" she shouts, her voice barely audible over the pounding bassline. It could be any party, in any town in the UK [United Kingdom]. The powder is ketamine, a Class C dissociative anaesthetic which is also used as a horse tranquilliser. When taken, it causes euphoria and powerful hallucinations, with users reporting out-of-body experiences and conversations with god.

A Fast-Growing Party Drug

In 2008 the British Crime Survey revealed it was the fastest growing "party drug" among 16–24-year-olds, leading it to be dubbed the "new ecstasy." It now boasts an estimated 125,000 users in the UK and more users among young people in England and Wales than heroin and crack cocaine combined.

But as the number of users rise, serious side effects are beginning to emerge. On internet forums for clubbers the stories all started the same. After about three months of regular use people were experiencing strange side effects; incontinence, blood in their urine and urine infections that did not respond to treatment.

By May 2008, doctors from the Bristol Urological Institute ("BUI") became concerned. They published a letter in the *British Medical Journal* reporting they had seen nine patients with severe urological symptoms associated with ketamine use over the last two years. The letter warned that these cases were "the tip of the iceberg." It was right. Since then, 15–20 people in the area have been put forward for bladder stretching, a surgical procedure performed under anaesthesia. Two users in their 20s had to have their bladders removed because they had incurred so much damage from the drug.

When you start using K it's very attractive, it's cheap and the effects are strong.

Daniel, a 21-year-old heavy user from Brighton knows his body is beyond repair. Doctors have told him that drug abuse has given him the bladder of an 80-year-old, and he needs to have it surgically stretched, but he cannot stop taking ketamine.

"I've got a fixation, I just think 'one more line.' I'll go for a piss, it will literally be a tablespoon's worth of urine. I'll piss out slugs of blood, like congealed jelly and the pain is horrific. It feels like a ball with loads of spikes just bouncing on your bladder. During a bad week I will go to the toilet every five minutes. I was in the job centre once having an interview and I had to stop halfway through because I was sitting there bursting."

Also known as K, special K and wonk, [it] can sell as cheaply as £6 per gram in the South West [England]. But few of its users will have heeded the warning on the government's drug website FRANK, of "serious bladder and related problems found in ketamine users."

There needs to [be] more preventative education about ketamine's effects.

An Epidemic That Destroys Bodies

Jess was 18 when she began taking ketamine. Two years later, she was wandering the streets of Bristol, high and covered in her own blood. Now 21, her health is a constant reminder of her drug use. She regularly suffers from cystitis because of the damage done to her bladder, and was hospitalised three times from kidney infections during her time on the drug. She also suffered from "k cramps", severe stomach pains associated with ketamine use. She says that the only cure for the cramps was taking more ketamine—trapping her in a vicious cycle of drug abuse and self harm: "It started off as very small amounts. When you start using K it's very attractive, it's cheap and the effects are strong."

A leaflet circulated by the Bristol Drugs Project (BDP) and the BUI to GPs [general practitioners] in the South West warns: "The symptoms can be severe enough to require hospitalisation ... and can result in irreversible bladder and renal damage. Although commoner among those who use ketamine daily or at high doses, it can also occur with lower dose recreational ketamine use."

The possibilities worry Jess, especially as she knows of 14- and 15-year-olds injecting the drug:

It's really, really scary. One of my friends got really wasted on ketamine and walked into the sea and drowned themself. It can have a massive effect on your mental state. When I was a heavy ketamine user I spent most of my time in my room on my own self-harming. I tried to give up many, many, many times. The only way I managed to do it was to get out of the country.

Dr Rachel Ayres, from the BDP, said urinary symptoms associated with ketamine use were becoming more widely known in the medical community as more people are abusing it:

"These problems are not due to contamination of ketamine, and they still develop even when you inject it rather than snort it. Some users think that damage is due to contaminated drugs but we think these problems are due to ketamine itself." Ayres emphasises that the users who had to have their bladders removed or stretched were at the severe end of the scale: "You have to be really bad to be referred to a urologist, and not everybody is."

Nate, 24 from Milton Keynes didn't go to see a doctor, even when he couldn't sleep through the night because he had to use the toilet so frequently. Charlie, 24, a student from Brighton also didn't seek help when he had the same problem. He says there needs to [be] more preventative education about ketamine's effects:

It's such a massive epidemic, it's something that you can get on any street corner. When ecstasy came onto the party scene there was a furore but there hasn't been for ketamine even though young people are destroying their bodies.

Young people like Emily, the 17-year-old at the squat party in Brighton who snorted the largest line. She's notorious on the Brighton party scene now—not for her hedonism or youthful charm, but for being incontinent.

Note: Some names have been changed.

7

Ketamine:
A Fast-Acting Antidepressant?

William M. Glazer

William M. Glazer is the president of Glazer Medical Solutions of Key West, Florida, and Menemsha, Massachusetts. He is a clinician, researcher, lecturer, and consultant and has been a faculty member of the psychiatry departments at the Yale and Harvard schools of medicine.

People who suffer from clinical depression have been helped with antidepressant medications currently on the market, like Prozac. The problem with these medications, however, is their slow response time; in some cases it can take weeks for patients to feel any beneficial effects. But recent studies incorporating the use of the drug ketamine have produced exciting results with patients experiencing relief from depression within two hours of treatment. While ketamine is known to cause some adverse side effects, such as urinary tract problems, researchers are hopeful that the new ketamine studies will lead to the rapid and successful long-term treatment of depression.

A revolutionary break-through in the treatment of depression occurred in the late 1950s with the discovery of the monoamine oxidase inhibitors and tricyclic antidepressants. Since then, newer agents, starting with Prozac, were introduced. These newer antidepressants had fewer side effects and thus were easier to prescribe and manage in patients.

But there has always been one concern about antidepressant medications: Even when effective, they have a slow onset of action. Typically, they take nine to 14 days to have any impact, and perhaps weeks to deliver their full effects, even as patients continue to endure painful symptoms, diminished functioning, and an increased suicide risk. But what if an antidepressant could offer a more rapid onset, with sustained antidepressant effects?

Research initiated at Yale University and later extended to the National Institute of Mental Health (NIMH) has explored the use of ketamine to help understand and address the delayed-onset action of currently available antidepressants.

Ketamine, which has been employed as a human and animal anesthetic, has been found to act in the human brain by blocking the N-methyl-D-aspartic acid (NMDA) receptor, which receives nerve signals carried by the neurotransmitter glutamate. Studies have suggested that dysregulation in glutamate activity could be a causative factor in depression.

Ketamine produced an antidepressant effect in 24 hours or less.

Ten years ago, investigators at Yale reported antidepressant effects of a single dose of intravenous (IV) ketamine in seven depressed patients. (1) Dr. John Krystal, who chairs the Department of Psychiatry at Yale University School of Medicine, has been studying ketamine since 1989 and was the senior author of that study. He found the antidepressant effect of ketamine extraordinary.

"It is simply striking to see someone who has struggled with long-standing treatment-resistant symptoms of depression get better overnight. It is a remarkable thing to see," Krystal says.

Six years following that Yale report, investigators at the NIMH replicated the results. (2) They reported "robust and rapid antidepressant effects" from a single intravenous dose of ketamine. The onset of action occurred within two hours after IV treatment and lasted one week. More recently, the NIMH investigators reported similar results when ketamine was added to lithium or valproate in bipolar depressed patients. (3) It appears that the rapid antidepressant effect of ketamine benefits about 70 percent of subjects who have participated in these studies.

Discovery: A "Faster" Neural Pathway

Scientists know that antidepressants act on specific targets called "receptors" in the cell membrane of a neuron that "listen" for signals from other neurons that are sent via neurotransmitters such as glutamate. When a neurotransmitter signal is received, receptors trigger a specific cascade of biochemical reactions within the neuron that enable it to respond to the signal. This is called a "signal transduction reaction." Typical antidepressant medications trigger reactions that ultimately take nine to 14 days to produce the desired antidepressant effect.

However, as noted, ketamine produced an antidepressant effect in 24 hours or less. This led experts to assume that ketamine's antidepressant effects occurred through a different and faster signal transduction chain. They theorized that if this faster pathway could be identified and understood, it might open the door to a new, faster way to treat depression.

A recent Yale University study, detailed in the August issue of *Science*, has validated the experts' assumption and identified the exact mechanism of ketamine's action. (4) In studies with rats, basic researchers observed that ketamine rapidly activates the "mammalian target of rapamycin" (mTOR) pathway, one of many such pathways that perform signal transduction in neurons. When the mTOR pathway was activated in rats, the Yale investigators observed an increase in synaptic signaling proteins, the number of new spinal dendrites, and motor activity that appeared consistent with animal models developed in antidepressant studies. Convincingly, these ketamine-induced changes did not occur when mTOR signaling was blocked.

Clinical Implications

These findings point to an exciting new direction for the treatment of depression: the potential for a 24-hour depression treatment. However, ketamine (or any other antidepressant that utilizes the mTOR pathway) would require a great deal of additional development before its use could be validated in routine clinical practice.

Ketamine is known to cause some undesirable cognitive and behavioral effects. Ravers in nightclubs abuse ketamine, or "Special K," to experience euphoria and perceptual distortions such as sounds and colors. Higher doses may produce outright hallucinations, delusions, and sometimes, paralysis. Recently, a study reported the occurrence of severe urinary tract dysfunction in long-term users of ketamine.

The work that went into the "ketamine story" has been a thing of beauty, and should be a source of hope to the millions who suffer from depression.

Despite these obstacles, Krystal feels that ketamine may yet be found feasible for clinical practice. "It may be that education, patient preparation, and initiation of other psychopharmacologic treatments to sustain remission will overcome these shortcomings, but this too has yet to be demonstrated," he says.

"At Yale," he adds, "we have conducted a preliminary open label study using ketamine for suicidal patients in a busy emergency room setting and it seemed quite feasible. The responses were encouraging." Krystal consults to several pharmaceutical companies and is a co-sponsor on two patent applications related to gluta-matergic treatments for mood and anxiety disorders, including one involving ketamine for depression.

Krystal points out that several issues suggest a high level of caution in incorporating ketamine into clinical practice:

- It is not clear how to transition someone from an acute antidepressant response lasting days to weeks to an extended remission. Ultimately, treatment is a long-term process and a rapid-onset antidepressant could play an important new role in inducing remission of depression that might help to reduce the impact of depression and avoid hospitalizations. "But, whether through repeated dosing or the initiation of other definitive treatments, it will be important to determine the best way to sustain the initial benefits," says Krystal.

- Some patients may not tolerate a rapid antidepressant treatment using ketamine.

- There is, at present, no way to determine which patients will be at higher risk for addiction to ketamine, given its prior history of abuse.

One More Piece of the Depression Puzzle

Yale's ketamine research effort represents years of collaboration between bench scientists (a group knowledgeable about brain mechanisms in animals) and clinicians knowledgeable about human psychiatric disorders. While a Yale faculty member, I witnessed this rare alliance between neuroscience and psychiatry and developed faith that knowledge about molecules will ultimately lead to the understanding and successful treatment of many psychiatric disorders. The work that went into the "ketamine story" has been a thing of beauty, and should be a source of hope to the millions who suffer from depression and the clinicians who treat them.

Now that activation of the mTOR pathway has been associated with the biochemical mechanism(s) of depression, scientists will be busy looking for simple blood tests to monitor mTOR activity and evaluating the antidepressant effects of other drugs that activate this pathway.

References

1. Berman RM, Cappiello A, Anand A, Oren D A, Heninger G R, Charney D S, Krystal J H. Antidepressant effects of ketamine in depressed patients. Biol Psychiatry. 2000 Feb 15; 47(4): 351–4.
2. Zarate C A, Singh J B, Carlson P J, et al. A Randomized Trial of an N-methyl-D-aspartate Antagonist in Treatment-Resistant Major Depression. Arch Gen Psychiatry. 2006; 63:856–864.
3. Diazgranados N, Ibrahim L, Brutsche N E, et al. A Randomized Add-on Trial of an N-methyl-D-aspartate Antagonist in Treatment-Resistant Bipolar Depression. Arch Gen Psychiatry. 2010; 67(8): 793–802.
4. Li N, Lee B, Liu R J, et al. mTOR-dependent synapse formation underlies the rapid antidepressant effects of NMDA antagonists. Science. 2010 Aug 20; 329(5994): 959–64.

8

The Use of Methamphetamine Can Devastate Lives

FRONTLINE

FRONTLINE is an investigative news and public affairs weekly television program that is distributed through the Public Broadcasting System (PBS).

The initial use of methamphetamine produces such a pleasurable, euphoric high that the user wants to experience that high again and again. Repeated use, however, ravages bodies and destroys lives. Researchers have found that methamphetamine profoundly impacts the brain's chemistry, resulting in potentially lifelong impairment of memory and motor coordination. Meth abuse also destroys tissue and blood vessels, increases heart rate, and can cause liver damage, convulsions, and stroke. What may be the most disastrous effect of all is the increased sex drive and resulting risky sexual behavior; the spread of Hepatitis B or C, HIV/AIDS, and even syphilis in some communities has been attributed to methamphetamine use.

What makes methamphetamine such an attractive high? Meth users report that after taking the drug they experience a sudden "rush" of pleasure or a prolonged sense of euphoria, as well as increased energy, focus, confidence, sexual prowess and feelings of desirability. However, after that first try, users require more and more of the drug to get that feeling again, and maintain it. With repeated use, methamphetamine exacts a toll on the mind and body, robbing users of their physical health and cognitive abilities, their libido and good looks, and their ability to experience pleasure. Here's how the body reacts to meth and the consequences of long-term abuse.

Meth Affects the Brain's Pleasure Center

- Meth releases a surge of dopamine, causing an intense rush of pleasure or prolonged sense of euphoria.

- Over time, meth destroys dopamine receptors, making it impossible to feel pleasure.

- Although these pleasure centers can heal over time, research suggests that damage to users' cognitive abilities may be permanent.

- Chronic abuse can lead to psychotic behavior, including paranoia, insomnia, anxiety, extreme aggression, delusions and hallucinations, and even death.

Meth, like all stimulants, causes the brain to release high doses of adrenaline, the body's "fight or flight" mechanism.

"There [are] a whole variety of reasons to try methamphetamine," explains Dr. Richard Rawson, associate director of UCLA's [University of California at Los Angeles] Integrated Substance Abuse Programs. "[H]owever, once they take the drug . . . their reasons are pretty much the same: They like how it affects their brain[s]." Meth users have described this feeling as a sudden rush of pleasure lasting for several minutes, followed by a euphoric high that lasts between six and 12 hours, and it is the result of [a] drug causing the brain to release excessive amounts of the chemical dopamine, a neurotransmitter that controls pleasure. All drugs of abuse cause the release of dopamine, even alcohol and nicotine, explains Rawson. "[But] methamphetamine produces the mother of all dopamine releases."

For example, in lab experiments done on animals, sex causes dopamine levels to jump from 100 to 200 units, and cocaine causes them to spike to 350 units. "[With] methamphetamine you get a release from the base level to about 1,250 units, something that's about 12 times as much of a release of dopamine as you get from food and sex and other pleasurable activities," Rawson says. "This really doesn't occur from any normally rewarding activity. That's one of the reasons why people, when they take methamphetamine, report having this euphoric [feeling] that's unlike anything they've ever experienced." Then, when the drug wears off, users experience profound depression and feel the need to keep taking the drug to avoid the crash.

Because meth causes the blood vessels to constrict, it cuts off the steady flow of blood to all parts of the body.

When addicts use meth over and over again, the drug actually changes their brain chemistry, destroying the wiring in the brain's pleasure centers and making it increasingly impossible to experience any pleasure at all. Although studies have shown that these tissues can regrow over time, the process can take years, and the repair may never be complete. A paper published by Dr. Nora Volkow, director of the National Institute on Drug Abuse, examines brain scans of several meth abusers who, after 14 months of abstinence from the drug, have regrown most of their damaged dopamine receptors; however, they showed no improvement in the cognitive abilities damaged by the drug. After more than a year's sobriety, these former meth users still showed severe impairment in memory, judgment and motor coordination, similar to symptoms seen in individuals suffering from Parkinson's Disease.

In addition to affecting cognitive abilities, these changes in brain chemistry can lead to disturbing, even violent behavior. Meth, like all stimulants, causes the brain to release high doses of adrenaline, the body's "fight or flight" mechanism, inducing anxiety, wakefulness and intensely focused attention, called "tweaking." When users are tweaking, they exhibit hyperactive and obsessive behavior, as journalist Thea Singer's sister Candy did on her meth binges. "When she was high, which was almost always, she had to be on the computer—diddling with programs to make them run faster, ordering freebies on the Internet," writes Singer [in her 2006 *Washington Post Magazine* article "Recipe for Disaster"]. "Then computers faded, and she was obsessed with diving into dumpsters—rescuing audio equipment from behind Radio Shack, pens from behind Office Depot." Heavy, chronic usage can also prompt psychotic behavior, such as paranoia, aggression, hallucinations and delusions. Some users have been known to feel insects crawling beneath their skin. "He picks and picks and picks at himself, like there are bugs inside his face," the mother of one meth addict told *The Spokesman-Review*. "He tears his clothes off and ties them around his head." The same article told the story of another former addict, who, even after five years of sobriety, can't go to the bathroom without propping a space heater against the door, in case someone is after him.

Meth Changes Physical Appearance

- Meth abuse causes the destruction of tissues and blood vessels, inhibiting the body's ability to repair itself.

- Acne appears, sores take longer to heal, and the skin loses its luster and elasticity, making the user appear years, even decades older.

- Poor diet, tooth grinding and oral hygiene results in tooth decay and loss.

One of the most striking effects of meth is the change in the physical appearance of meth users. Because meth causes the blood vessels to constrict, it cuts off the steady flow of blood to all parts of the body. Heavy usage can weaken and destroy these vessels, causing tissues to become prone to damage and inhibiting the body's ability to repair itself. Acne appears, sores take longer to heal, and the skin loses its luster and elasticity. Some users are covered in small sores, the result of obsessive skin-picking brought on by the hallucination of having bugs crawling beneath the skin, a disorder known as formication.

In addition, stimulants such as meth cause tremendous bursts of physical activity while suppressing the appetite, an attractive combination for many people who began using meth to lose weight. But while contemporary culture may idealize slim figures, heavy meth users often become gaunt and frail. Their day- or week-long meth "runs" are usually accompanied by tooth-grinding, poor diet, and bad hygiene, which lead to mouths full of broken, stained and rotting teeth.

A common sign of meth abuse is extreme tooth decay.

While a meth high makes users feel more confident, attractive, and desirable, the drug is actually working to make them unattractive. "Some people I have in here over a hundred times, and I can look over a 10, 15, 20-year period and see how they've deteriorated, how they've changed," says Deputy Brett King, from Oregon's Multnomah County Sheriff's Department. "Some were quite attractive when they began to come to jail: young people who were full of the health and had everything going for them . . . and now they're a shell of what they once were." Curious about this particular effect of the drug, King began collecting mug shots of individuals who had been booked repeatedly with meth in their blood. One of the faces that made a particular impression on him was that of Theresa Baxter: "She came in, and she was quite visibly intoxicated by methamphetamine. She looked horrible. She looked at least 20 years older than she was. Her teeth were missing, and I looked back in her history, and at one time she was a fairly attractive young woman."

Meth Use Creates "Meth Mouth"

- "Meth mouth" is characterized by broken, discolored and rotting teeth.

- The drug causes the salivary glands to dry out, which allows the mouth's acids to eat away at the tooth enamel, causing cavities.

- Teeth are further damaged when users obsessively grind their teeth, binge on sugary food and drinks, and neglect to brush or floss for long periods of time.

A common sign of meth abuse is extreme tooth decay, a condition that has become known in the media as "meth mouth." Users with "meth mouth" have blackened, stained, or rotting teeth, which often can't be saved, even among young or short-term users. The exact causes of "meth mouth" are not fully understood. Various reports have attributed the decay to the corrosive effects of the chemicals found in the drug, such as anhydrous ammonia (found in fertilizers), red phosphorus (found on matchboxes) and lithium (found in batteries), which when smoked or snorted might erode the tooth's protective enamel coating; however, it's more likely that this degree of tooth decay is brought on by a combination of side effects from a meth high.

When meth is ingested, it causes the user's blood vessels to shrink, limiting the steady blood supply that the mouth needs in order to stay healthy. With repeated shrinking, these vessels die and the oral tissues decay. Similarly, meth use leads to "dry mouth" (xerostomia), and without enough saliva to neutralize the mouth's harsh acids, those acids eat away at the tooth and gums, causing weak spots that are susceptible to cavities. The cavities are then exacerbated by behavior common in users on a meth high: a strong desire for sugary foods and drinks, compulsive tooth grinding, and the general neglect of regular brushing and flossing.

> *One of the most dangerous effects of meth on the body is the increase in sex drive and the lowering of sexual inhibitions among some users, which puts them at risk for sexually transmitted diseases.*

The extent of tooth decay varies widely among meth users. A 2000 report in the *Journal of Periodontology* found that users who snorted the drug had significantly worse tooth decay than users who smoked or injected it, although all types of users suffered from dental problems. Anecdotal evidence also suggests that the degree of tooth decay is not necessarily dependent on the length of drug use. "[O]ne gentleman I saw said he used it for four months and there was nothing except for root tips left in his mouth," said Dr. Athena Bettger, a dentist who practices two days a week at the Multnomah County Jail in Portland, Ore. "Whereas another gentleman I saw said he was using it for four years, and . . . I think three teeth needed to come out and he needed a couple of fillings because of the cavities."

Dentists like Dr. Bettger, who practice in America's prisons and jails, have seen some of the worst cases of "meth mouth," and state correctional facilities are feeling the impact on their budgets. In August 2005, National Public Radio [NPR] reported that dental costs in the Minnesota Department of Corrections had doubled in the past five years, mostly due to the extensive dental work performed on former meth addicts. Although there are no quantitative studies to document this phenomenon, anecdotal evidence supports this trend. Dr. Chris Heringlake, a dentist at St. Cloud Correctional Facility in Minnesota, told NPR that he first saw "meth mouth" eight years ago, and now he sees it every day. Dr. Bettger has also noticed this trend in Oregon: "The general trend that I am seeing is that there is a definite increase. . . . There are more and more teeth that need assistance and there are more and more [inmates] needing assistance."

Meth Use Can Lead to Risky Sexual Behavior

- Meth heightens the libido and impairs judgment, which can lead to risky sexual behavior.

- Many users take the drug intravenously, increasing their chances of contracting diseases such as Hepatitis B or C and HIV/AIDS.

One of the most dangerous effects of meth on the body is the increase in sex drive and the lowering of sexual inhibitions among some users, which puts them at risk for sexually transmitted diseases. Although meth is not necessarily an aphrodisiac, it does trigger the release of powerful brain chemicals that may increase sex drive, such as dopamine, which gives the user a sense of well-being and desirability, and adrenaline, which provides the user with a boost in confidence and stamina. Meanwhile, these chemicals impair the judgment centers of the brain. "You do things when you're on meth that you would never do sober," explains Peter Staley, a former meth user. "You drop your guard. Condoms? Forget about it." Unprotected sex is particularly dangerous for meth users, many of whom inject the drug and may share needles, which can spread deadly diseases such as hepatitis and HIV. Also, because the drug increases energy and stamina, users may have more aggressive sex for longer periods of time, increasing the chances of injury and the danger of spreading infection.

In New York's gay community, where meth has been popular since the late 1990s, it has contributed to an increase in infections of HIV/AIDS, which, until recently had been declining. "In New York, we're seeing about 1,000 gay men every year become infected, and that's just unacceptable," says Staley, now an anti-meth activist in the gay community. "It's very sad. It's tragic, and it's almost entirely because of crystal meth." But the meth-related spread of disease is not limited to urban gay communities; anyone engaging in risky sexual behavior or the sharing of needles is highly susceptible. In Oregon, the prevalence of crystal meth, which is often taken intravenously, is thought to be the cause of a recent rise in syphilis cases, and state health officials fear that it might lead to a boom in cases of HIV. "Whether you have a history of drug addiction or not, has no bearing on whether you get addicted to this drug," Staley tells *FRONTLINE*. "It is Russian roulette, pure and simple. And for a large portion of those who try it, their lives get destroyed."

Meth's cruel irony is that while it increases sexual desire and stamina, it ultimately decreases the user's sexual desirability and performance. Chronic, heavy use of the drug destroys the user's good looks and leads to impotence, known in some gay circles as "crystal dick." Other users report the inability to reach an orgasm at all, despite maintaining arousal for long periods of time. And some users, such as journalist Thea Singer's sister, Candy, lose interest in sex altogether, as meth becomes the sole focus of their lives: "Sex interfered with my drug use," she says.

Meth's Other Effects on the Body

- Increased heart rate

- Disorganized lifestyle

- Lowered resistance to illness

- Liver damage

- Convulsions

- Extreme rise in body temperature, which can cause brain damage

- Stroke

- Death

9

The Drug "Spice"
May Be Harmful and
Should Be Regulated

Heidi Toth

Heidi Toth is a journalist and news reporter for the Utah newspaper, the Daily Herald.

A new drug is becoming popular among teenage users because the high is similar to that of marijuana and it is legal and readily available. The drug—called "spice"—is sold as herbal incense and carries the warning "not for human consumption," making it legal to buy and sell without regulation by the Food and Drug Administration (FDA). And since it is not regulated, no one knows exactly what components are in spice or how the drug will affect the body in the short and long term. It is known, however, that smoking spice aggressively affects receptors in the brain; reported side effects include numbness in the body, slurred speech, chest pain, vomiting, coma, and seizures.

Smoking marijuana may not destroy your life like a heroin addiction or damage your body like cocaine. It does, however, destroy trust and damage relationships; no parent wants to be lied to, to lay awake at night wondering what's going on with their children or to explain to a 5-year-old girl why her brother isn't around much anymore and doesn't seem to like his family very much.

Now, a new substance that mimics the effects of marijuana is sold legally as an incense. It could be causing the same worries—except most parents have no idea that the marijuana substitute even exists. They don't know what signs to watch for. They don't recognize the smell. It's sold by legitimate businesses and does not show up in drug tests.

A Legal Marijuana Substitute

This drug, known genetically as spice, sort of looks like and sort of acts like pot. But in some ways, it is drastically different, and no one knows exactly what to look for or what to do now that it's here. Because it's so new, there are more questions than answers on the long-term effects of its usage and what regulation, if any, is needed; part of the ongoing debate at the county and state levels is if anything should be done.

Almost anyone could walk into a smoke shop or convenience store and buy the product, which is a drug no matter how it's marketed.

For some, the answer is an unequivocal yes. Law enforcement officials want to get the word out that teenagers are using spice and get regulation of some kind in place to curtail its use.

"Anything to curb the use of this stuff," said Sgt. Wayne Keith, who runs a canyon patrol for the Utah County Sheriff's Office. "I think a lot of parents out there and the public have no idea what's going on."

He said spice is showing up more and more at parties in place of marijuana. He wants people to be aware that this drug use is happening, that it's happening in Utah County and that almost anyone could walk into a smoke shop or convenience store and buy the product, which is a drug no matter how it's marketed, he said.

"The biggest reason for me is I see all the young kids out getting—I don't know what other word to use except stoned—on this stuff," Keith [said].

The same goes for the parents of one south Utah County young adult who have watched almost helplessly as their talented 20-year-old son who says he wants to be a doctor sleeps his life away except for when he's smoking spice two or three times a day since sometime after Thanksgiving, when he came home early from his LDS [Latter Day Saints] mission.

"(He) felt like it was OK for him to do that because it's not illegal," his father said. "It needs to be illegal. Why would you not make it illegal when it's the same as marijuana?"

Not Intended for Human Consumption

A clerk at a smoke shop answers questions about spice easily and gestures toward the large selection of the incense, which displays the different jar sizes, the flavors and the brands that don't contain acetone, an industrial solvent used to clean labs and remove nail polish. They don't sell the product to anyone younger than 19 years old, he says, and points out that each bottle is clearly labeled "not for human consumption."

Because spice is ostensibly sold as incense, it goes unregulated by the Food and Drug Administration, much like candles or Glade Plug-Ins.

The clerk pauses, leaving the unspoken reality lingering in the air with the pungent aroma of a dozen different types of tobacco—it's not like that label has stopped anybody. "I tried it," he says.

The clerk, A.N., asked not to be identified because of the sensitive nature of the subject. He said he'd smoked the herbal incense twice; the first time was an experiment, the second time because he remembered what the first time felt like. "I was just trying to freaking get away from the stress, because I'd had a long day, you know?" A.N. said.

Because spice is ostensibly sold as incense, it goes unregulated by the Food and Drug Administration [FDA], much like candles or Glade Plug-Ins.

But no one is pouring oil from a Plug-In into a bong and lighting up to get high. Likewise, almost no one is buying or has ever bought spice because it smells good. A.N., who works at a smoke shop in northern Utah County, said when customers come in and ask him for the good stuff, they're not asking for the best aroma. They're asking for the best high.

"We guide them to what is strong stuff," he said.

Customers ask what burns the best and the quickest, what's smooth or harsh, what kind of effects the different brands have. They ask about the legality of smoking spice. But A.N. doesn't remember a single customer who has asked about health issues related to ingesting a product that was never designed or tested for ingestion. "They already know what it is," he said. "They don't even ask those questions. They just come get it. . . . They just like to get high."

Dr. Micah Smith, an emergency room doctor at Timpanogos Regional Hospital in Orem [Utah], says he has no doubt that every vendor of this product knows customers will be smoking it. They use the incense label just to get around FDA regulations, he said. "The folks that were selling it were knowingly selling it as an abused product," Smith said. "That's the bothersome part."

A.N. knows what customers do with the spice when they leave the store; they are, after all, selling products that are meant to be smoked. Other store managers disagree. A manager at The Hookah Garden in American Fork [Utah], who declined to give his name, said they do not sell spice for smoking purposes, and if clerks suspect it is being used as a drug, they are instructed to not sell it to that customer.

Brandon Bigler, the general manager at Stogies Smoke Shop in Provo [Utah], said customers ask general questions about smoking spice; he and the staff respond that they don't know how people use the product. He does, however, have suspicions about how regular spice buyers use their purchases. "I do, but I don't ever really try to entertain those suspicions," he said. "I just sell it. People do with it what they want when they're out of the store."

Out of almost a dozen convenience stores the *[Daily] Herald* asked, only a couple sold spice, although almost all of the clerks knew what it was.

Deputy Jay Lessley, a drug recognition expert for the sheriff's office, said the product's actual use is obvious; store owners choose to downplay their liability by touting that spice is not for human consumption. People wouldn't spend $30 on a product that makes their houses smell like burnt grass, he said. "I just don't know how they couldn't suspect something's up," Lessley said.

The Effects of Smoking Spice

The biggest problem with spice is the uncertainty factor. Without studies, no one can accurately predict the body's response over a long time.

In the short term, spice interacts with the same cannabinoid receptors in the brain that marijuana does, Lessley said. He has been told that the brain is actually about five times more receptive to the synthetic cannabinoids than to THC [the active ingredient] in marijuana. These chemicals are more aggressive in how they work with the brain, he said. This results in a high similar to marijuana, although some have reported it to be more intense and almost all have reported that it doesn't last as long. "It looks just like, from what I've seen, somebody under the influence of marijuana," [said] Lessley.

Typically, users display similar physiological reactions from spice impairment as with marijuana impairment: loss of cognition, slow response time, inability to pay attention, dilated pupils, reddened tissues around the eyes and elevated pulse and blood pressure. But in just enough cases to be worrisome, the high isn't anything like marijuana or anything like health professionals expect.

> The side effects [of spice] reported to the [Utah Poison Control Center] included slurred speech, agitation, paranoia, chest pain, vomiting, tachycardia, coma and seizures.

Dr. Smith has treated two patients in the last four months who told him they'd smoked spice. Both were men in their 20s. One was sedated and confused. The other was "crawling out of his skin and crazy"; he was agitated, confused, in need of sedation—not hallucinating but "definitely in a different plane than the rest of us," Smith said. He'd never heard of it before the first man came into the emergency room [ER], he said. Other people may be using it and not 'fessing up at the ER.

Users reported a different high than marijuana, although it had some similarities. A.N., who's smoked spice twice but never marijuana, said some brands gave a "brain high"—he couldn't concentrate on conversations or movies or focus on anything. "It gets you high in a way that makes you laugh," he said. "You don't even remember what you're saying." He laughed about everything, almost to the point that he felt like his heart was going to stop beating from all the laughing, he said.

The other time he had a "body high"—numbness, a feeling of disconnectedness from the body. A.N. said his body went numb starting at the feet and moving up. Holli Butler, a 19-year-old Payson, [Utah] woman, described it as a calming of all the nerves and muscles minus the floating feeling or mental dumbness of marijuana.

The Utah Poison Control Center has had 21 calls about spice or synthetic marijuana since November [2009]. Marty Malheiro said the side effects reported to the center included slurred speech, agitation, paranoia, chest pain, vomiting, tachycardia, coma and seizures. Many of those are similar to marijuana; a few are the opposite of what marijuana should do.

Dr. Greg Hanson, director of the Utah Addiction Center, said THC actually has an antinausea effect and is used medicinally for that reason. Spice users also have reported upset stomach and diarrhea, which is not at all like marijuana; this suggests to him there is more in those little bottles than is listed. Marijuana also often results in paranoia among users. Paranoia wasn't listed as a possible effect of spice, but the drug sometimes had other mental effects that made people act out, like the second man Smith treated in his hospital.

It's still a mood-altering drug that may make users act unpredictably.

One such incident of this kind of response was in 18-year-old David Rozga of Indianola, Iowa. He killed himself on June 6, [2010] just a little while after getting high on spice. According to the police report, he and a couple of friends smoked K2, and Rozga then "freaked out" and told his friends he was going to hell or was in hell. Then he told his friends he was going to go home and rest. He went home and shot himself. Two of his friends told police they didn't know why Rozga would kill himself; another friend's mother said he was depressed and had talked about suicide before.

The police had not received results from the medical examiner's office to determine how much of the substance was in Rozga's body when he died.

"It's Legal and It's Available"

Spice does not show up in drug tests, and there likely won't be any tests for it soon because increasing the number of drugs screened for significantly increases the cost of a test and won't be affordable for companies, said Rick Visser, a counselor for the Alcohol and Chemical Treatment Center at Ogden Regional Medical Center.

This also means spice is legally acceptable for drug court participants, who typically are told to stay away from all drugs, including alcohol. However, since there is no test and no law, it's a non-issue. Visser said the drug courts generally are waiting for the legal system to catch up. Judge James Taylor, who oversees drug court for the 4th District Court in Utah County, said nothing has come up with any screenings and spice use has no impact on the court.

Butler and Terrin Memmott, also 19 and of Payson, started using spice as a substitute for pot. They both got misdemeanor charges for possession of marijuana earlier this year, and when Butler learned about spice in the smoke shop where she buys cigarettes, they tried it. "We've been smoking spice since then," she said. "We used the spice to get off the marijuana."

It's still a mood-altering drug that may make users act unpredictably and does who-knows-what in the long term. Keith said that, like any drug, spice is not safe, which is what's driving the county's push to learn more about it and then determine what to do with it.

Health officials don't see much of a risk of addiction with spice; similarly, there is little chance of getting addicted to marijuana. A.N., who has some customers in the store almost daily to get spice, said addiction could be a factor in people's use, but he didn't think that motivated his customers. "It's a habit," he said. "People don't want to drop it."

He said spice has two main draws: it's legal and it's available. People don't need to worry about getting caught using it or sneaking around trying to buy it.

As much as it pains many of them to say it, most health professionals recognize that people who want to get high will find ways to get high, Smith, the ER doctor, said.

10

Use of the Drug "Spice" Is Causing Concern in the Military

Julie Watson

Julie Watson is a staff writer for the Associated Press.

A new synthetic drug that is comparable to marijuana but with a more intense and potentially harmful high is called "spice," and its use is becoming increasingly popular among military personnel. Although the drug is bought and sold legally because it is marketed as incense or potpourri, the military has a zero-tolerance policy for drugs and does not allow its use. Spice is difficult to detect, however, because over two hundred chemicals are used in the product, and makers of drug tests are unable to keep up with manufacturers' adaptations. Of further concern is the drug's effects on people, such as vomiting, seizures, anxiety, and delusions—symptoms that are especially dangerous in the military environment.

U.S. troops are increasingly using an easy-to-get herbal mix called "spice," which mimics a marijuana high, is hard to detect and can bring on hallucinations that last for days. The abuse of the substance has so alarmed military officials that they've launched an aggressive testing program that this year [2011] has led to the investigation of more than 1,100 suspected users.

So-called "synthetic" pot is readily available on the Internet and has become popular nationwide in recent years, but its use among troops and sailors has raised concerns among the Pentagon brass.

"You can just imagine the work that we do in a military environment," said Mark Ridley, deputy director of the Naval Criminal Investigative Service. "You need to be in your right mind when you do a job. That's why the Navy has always taken a zero-tolerance policy toward drugs."

Two years ago, only 29 Marines and sailors were investigated for spice use. This year, the number topped 700, the investigative service said. Those found guilty of using spice are kicked out, although the Navy does not track the overall number of dismissals.

The Air Force has punished 497 airmen so far this year, compared with last year's 380, according to Pentagon figures. The Army does not track spice investigations but says it has medically treated 119 soldiers negatively affected by the synthetic drug.

More than 40 states have banned some of its chemicals, prompting sellers to turn to the Internet, where spice is marketed as incense or potpourri.

Military officials emphasize those caught represent a tiny fraction of all service members and note none was in a leadership position or believed high while on duty.

Spice is made up of exotic plants from Asia like Blue Lotus and Bay Bean. Their leaves are coated with chemicals that mimic the effects of THC, the active ingredient in marijuana, but are five to 200 times more potent.

More than 40 states have banned some of its chemicals, prompting sellers to turn to the Internet, where spice is marketed as incense or potpourri. In some states, spice is sold at bars, smoke shops and convenience stores. . . .

The packets often say the ingredients are not for human consumption and are for aromatherapy. They are described as "mood enhancing" and "long lasting." Some of the sellers' websites say they do not sell herbal mixes containing any illegal chemicals and say they are offering a "legal high." Service members preferred it because, up until this year, there was no way to detect it with urine tests.

Emergency crews have responded to calls of "hyper-excited" people doing things like tearing off their clothes and running down the street naked.

A test was developed after the Drug Enforcement Administration put a one-year emergency ban on five chemicals found in the drug. Manufacturers are adapting to avoid detection, even on the new tests, and skirt new laws banning the main chemicals, officials say. "It's a moving target," said Capt. J.A. "Cappy" Surette, spokesman for the Navy Bureau of Medicine and Surgery.

The military can calibrate its equipment to test for those five banned chemicals, "but underground chemists can keep altering the properties and make up to more than 100 permutations," Surette said. Complicating the military's efforts further, there are more than 200 other chemicals used in the concoctions. They remain legal, and their effects on the mind and body remain largely unknown, Navy doctors say. A Clemson University scientist created many of the chemicals for research purposes in 1990s. They were never tested on humans.

Civilian deaths have been reported and emergency crews have responded to calls of "hyper-excited" people doing things like tearing off their clothes and running down the street naked. Navy investigators compare the substance to angel dust because no two batches are the same. Some who smoke it like a marijuana cigarette may just feel a euphoric buzz, but others have suffered delusions lasting up to a week.

While the problem has surfaced in all branches of the military, the Navy has been the most aggressive in drawing attention to the problem. It produced a video based on cases to warn sailors of spice's dangers and publicized busts of crew members on some of its most-storied ships, including the *USS Carl Vinson*, from which Osama bin Laden's body was dropped into the sea.

Two of the largest busts this year involved sailors in the San Diego-based U.S. Third Fleet, which announced last month [November 2011] that it planned to dismiss 28 sailors assigned to the aircraft carrier *USS Ronald Reagan*. A month earlier, 64 sailors, including 49 from the *Vinson*, were accused of being involved in a spice ring. Many of the cases were discovered after one person was caught with synthetic pot, prompting broader investigations.

Lt. Commander Donald Hurst, a fourth-year psychiatry resident at San Diego's Naval Medical Center, said the hospital is believed to have seen more cases than any other health facility in the country. Once a month, doctors saw users experiencing bad reactions, but now see them weekly. Users suffer everything from vomiting, elevated blood pressure and seizures to extreme agitation, anxiety and delusions. Hurst said the behavior in many cases he witnessed at first seemed akin to schizophrenia. Usually within minutes, however, the person became completely lucid. Sometimes, the person goes in and out of such episodes for days.

He recalled one especially bizarre case of a sailor who came in with his sobbing wife. "He stood there holding a sandwich in front of him with no clue as to what to do," he said. "He opened it up, looked at it, touched it. I took it and folded it over and then he took a bite out it. But then we had to tell him, 'You have to chew.'" An hour later, when Hurst went back to evaluate the man, he was completely normal and worried about being in trouble. "That's something you don't see with acute schizophrenic patients," Hurst said.

Hurst decided to study 10 cases. Some also had smoked marijuana or drank alcohol, while others only smoked spice. Of the 10, nine had lost a sense of reality. Seven babbled incoherently. The symptoms for seven of them lasted four to eight days. Three others are believed to now be schizophrenic. Hurst believed the drug may have triggered the symptoms in people with that genetic disposition. His findings were published in the *American Journal of Psychiatry* in October. He said there are countless questions that still need answering, including the designer drug's effects on people with post-traumatic stress disorder or traumatic brain injuries. What the research has confirmed, he said, is: "These are not drugs to mess with."

11

Taking Drugs Known as Bath Salts Can Cause Serious Health Consequences

Niki D'Andrea

Niki D'Andrea, associate editor at Phoenix *magazine and a blogger at* The Phoenix Edge, *was also a staff writer at the* Phoenix New Times.

A new craze among drug users nationwide is smoking, snorting, or injecting "bath salts," a product that is sold legally over the Internet or in head shops because it is marketed as a toiletry and labeled "not for human consumption." Even though these so-called bath salts are legal, they are not safe to use. In fact, the Federal Drug Enforcement Administration (DEA) reported that these drugs are mixed with chemical compounds similar to the illegal compounds found in ecstasy and methamphetamine. Furthermore, police and medical professionals are seeing serious health consequences from ingesting bath salts, including seizures, chest pains, dizziness, vomiting, paranoia, and even suicidal tendencies.

The hottest new drug on the streets is perfectly legal—and totally dangerous, according to everyone from the DEA [Drug Enforcement Administration] to local toxicology experts.

Sold on the Internet and at head shops under names such as Ivory Wave, Cloud 9, Vanilla Sky, and White Lightning, "bath salts" sound so sweet and innocent. But the alleged potent effects of these particular bath salts don't come from dumping them in the tub for a relaxing soak. The packets contain small amounts of white crystalline powder, and they're labeled with warnings like "novelty only" and "not for human consumption."

Legal Drugs That Resemble Illegal Drugs

But there have been more than a hundred reports nationwide of people smoking, snorting, eating, or injecting the bath salts—with ill effects ranging from paranoia to seizures. Doing so is said to produce effects similar to highs from ecstasy (heightening of the senses, sexual arousal) and stimulants like cocaine and methamphetamine (euphoria and increased energy). . . .

The bath salts are being sold widely—and legally, for now—in the United States. They are marketed here much in the same manner as "herbal incense" (also called spice). Spice was sold for "aromatherapy only" and also labeled "not for human consumption," but chemical compounds sprayed on the herbs (five of which were federally banned in December [2010]) replicated a marijuana high when people smoked it. Spice blends are still sold in head shops, but they don't have the banned compounds in them anymore.

Side effects of snorting bath salts include increased heart rate and chest pain, agitation and paranoia, dizziness and vomiting, and profuse sweating.

The speedy high from ingesting bath salts is said to come from two synthetic compounds, mephedrone and methylene-dioxypyrovalerone (MDPV). The federal Drug Enforcement Administration was alerted to their presence in 2009, when they showed up in lab tests on substances seized by law enforcement officers in six states. Last year [2010], the DEA published reports on both compounds, noting that each was "related in chemical structure" to illegal hallucinogenic substances like MDMA (ecstasy) and illegal stimulants like cathinone and methamphetamine.

Mephedrone, first synthesized and reported in a French academic journal in 1929, didn't appear on the designer drug market until 2003, when an underground chemist named Kinetic rediscovered and published the formula on the website The Hive (the site shut down in 2004). It's been banned in numerous places, including Israel and Europe. MDPV has reportedly been sold as a "research chemical" since 2008. It has been banned in Finland, Denmark, and Sweden. Neither compound is currently a federally controlled substances in the United States, which makes "bath salts" containing them legal to buy and sell—but far from perfectly safe.

Questionable Ingredients That Pose Serious Health Risks

Side effects of snorting bath salts include increased heart rate and chest pain, agitation and paranoia, dizziness and vomiting, and profuse sweating. Poison-control centers around the country have reported receiving more than 160 calls about bath salts in the past three months. Much of the buzz has come from Louisiana, where at least 84 people have been hospitalized after ingesting them. . . .

Dr. Daniel Brooks, co-medical director of the Department of Medical Toxicology at the Banner Good Samaritan Poison and Drug Information Center in Phoenix [Arizona], is familiar with mephedrone and MDPV as "relatively novel synthetic stimulants" but says that little academic research has been done on them and that they've never been tested on humans. Medical professionals aren't 100 percent certain how these compounds are metabolized or how they'll react with other drugs. The ingredients in bath salts aren't listed on the packages, so users have no way of knowing what they're actually ingesting.

You get all revved up and your temperature can go up to 103, 104, 105 degrees, and that can lead to seizures and liver disease and kidney disease.

"We see patients that are often sent to us after overdoses and adverse drug effects. I don't have specific numbers and such, but a lot of the patients that come to us saying they bought an illicit substance, like . . . spice or mephedrone; especially these newer drugs that are out on the market, we often run tests and find other drugs in their system," Brooks says. "I think that's the main problem with using illicit substances. Anything that's not regulated . . . you never know what you're getting. They could say it's spice, but it's really methamphetamine. Or they can say it's mephedrone, but it's some prescription anti-psychotic."

"There's a risk of having to trust your supplier—and who knows who your supplier is?—or their ability to make these compounds," Brooks says. "It's always pretty much clandestine labs set up in a trailer or an apartment or a house—or wherever they're making these things—and just distributing them with or without adulterants."

"The big risk of adverse effects [with stimulants] always occurs in the dose, and how much you take, and the concentration, which you may not know," Brooks says. One risk of using synthetic speed in Phoenix is hyperthermia. "You get all revved up and your temperature can go up to 103, 104, 105 degrees, and that can lead to seizures and liver disease and kidney disease."

But Brooks adds that most of the time, "these drugs can be treated with basic supportive care," and he hasn't seen a lot of cases of extremely sick mephedrone and MDPV users in Arizona.

Costly Toiletries That Cost Lives

Other states haven't been so lucky. Last month [December 2010] in Kansas, 21-year-old Elijah Taylor ran onto Interstate 135, waving his hands, before he was struck and killed by a van. In his pocket, police discovered a container of Blue Magic Bath Salts. Toxicology tests are pending.

In October 2010, 29-year-old Jarrod Moody committed suicide in Missouri, allegedly after a binge on Ivory Wave bath salts. Moody had reportedly been off painkillers for two years when he developed an addiction to Ivory Wave. His father told media he found several packets of the bath salts in his son's room. Moody's friends and family described him as emaciated, paranoid, and sleepless in the days leading to his death.

Although mephedrone and MDPV are not currently controlled in the United States, both were placed on the DEA's list of "Drugs and Chemicals of Concern" last year. And possession or use of substances containing them and sold for human consumption could be prosecuted under the Federal Analog Act.

Analogs are chemical compounds derived from another compound, which often differ by a single element. Mephedrone and MDVP are both analogs of cathinone, a chemical similar to amphetamine and derived from the khat plant. Cathinone has been illegal internationally since the 1971 Convention on Psychotropic Substances in Austria.

Because they involve analogs of a controlled substance, law enforcement cases involving mephedrone and MDPV can be prosecuted under the Federal Analog Act—if the substances were intended for human consumption. But the bath salts believed to contain these compounds are marketed and sold strictly as toiletries—and they're the most expensive on the market. Considering that 20 ounces of regular bath salts sells for about $7 on Amazon.com, the bath salts sold in head shops for as much as $120 a gram make a ridiculously expensive soak in the tub.

12

Community Coalitions Can Help Reduce Access to Synthetic Drugs

Erica Leary

Erica Leary is the program manager for the North Coastal Prevention Coalition (NCPC) located in north San Diego County, California. She has given presentations at various local, state, and national trainings and conferences on prevention strategies and community coalition efforts to reduce the use of alcohol, tobacco, marijuana, and other drugs in communities of San Diego County.

Products containing synthetic marijuana-like chemicals that are legally sold in stores and on the Internet as herbal incense—such as Spice, K2, or bath salts—are presenting challenges for communities across the nation in their efforts to combat drug abuse. For example, synthetic drug use has seriously impacted high school campuses, adolescent treatment centers, and the military sector in California's San Diego County. But youth councils and community coalition groups in San Diego are fighting back with outreach, education, and training programs. Such coalitions and collaborative efforts are vital in order to reduce the sale and distribution of these dangerous products.

I am here today on behalf of the North Coastal Prevention Coalition, which serves the cities of Vista, Oceanside, and Carlsbad in north San Diego County [California], but will

Erica Leary, "The Dangers of Synthetic Cannabinoids and Stimulants," Testimony Before the Senate Caucus on International Narcotics Control, CADCA.org, March 4, 2011. Copyright © 2011 by Erica Leary. All rights reserved. Reproduced by permission.

also share findings and experiences from several colleagues throughout San Diego County who share our concerns regarding synthetic drugs, and support efforts to address this problem....

We recognize that access and availability of drugs (including alcohol) are key factors in rates of use, and have led numerous successful efforts to reduce availability of alcohol and other drugs to youth. However, products containing synthetic cannabinoids have presented us with a new challenge as they've spread to various retail outlets under the false pretense of being "incense," and are viewed as a legal alternative to marijuana use by teens and others.

Today [March 4, 2011], I'll be sharing with you some examples of how synthetic marijuana products have impacted various sectors in San Diego County; where we are finding these products, and how they are marketed; some recent efforts undertaken to address the problem; and how this proposed legislation may be utilized at the local level to help eliminate these dangerous products in our communities.

It appears synthetic marijuana use has impacted many sectors throughout San Diego County, including high school campuses, adolescent treatment centers, probation, and the military.

The Impact of Synthetic Marijuana Is Extensive

Our coalition first became aware of Spice and similar products approximately 18 months ago when a colleague who coordinates an after-school program asked us what we knew about this new legal marijuana-like product that many teens in his program were discussing. Several had tried it, and since it was being sold in local stores, they assumed it was legal and safe, and that they couldn't get in trouble for using it.

In speaking with colleagues throughout San Diego County, products like Spice appeared on the radar in 2009 and increased substantially in 2010. Comprehensive data is not available for several reasons: our student surveys are only conducted every two years and do not currently ask specific questions regarding products like Spice; drug tests for synthetic marijuana have only recently been developed and are currently too expensive to conduct on a routine basis; and current systems impacted by the use of synthetic marijuana, such as emergency rooms, treatment programs, and criminal justice, have not had time to change their existing data collection processes to single out the specific impact of Spice and similar products.

However, through anecdotal evidence, it appears synthetic marijuana use has impacted many sectors throughout San Diego County, including high school campuses, adolescent treatment centers, probation, and the military.

Alcohol and marijuana use remain the primary drugs of choice for adolescents in our area, but Spice is viewed as a convenient alternative, especially for those who are likely to be subjected to random drug tests. A clinical social worker with the Marine Corps Substance Abuse Counseling Center in San Diego informed me that they first learned of Spice use by finding drug paraphernalia. When drug tests of those in possession of paraphernalia turned up negative, they confessed to smoking Spice. Similarly, some clients in residential or outpatient adolescent treatment programs admit to using Spice after their drug tests turn out negative, despite exhibiting signs of being under the influence. Joe Olesky, a substance abuse counselor with the San Dieguito Union High School District and coordinator of the READI Program (Recovery Education Alcohol Drug Initiative), noted that they've had 8–10 parents very concerned that drug tests they administered to their teens have come out positive for PCP. The teens then admitted to using Spice as an alternative to marijuana. Mr. Olesky believes this may explain the often erratic behavior and hallucinations those using Spice describe.

Drug testing manufacturers have since developed new tests capable of detecting synthetic marijuana products, but they remain significantly more expensive than standard tests. I have been told that when these new tests have been piloted in various settings, such as juvenile probation or treatment programs, the positive rate is significant, sometimes with over half the tests administered coming back positive for synthetic THC [the active ingredient in marijuana].

> Unlike some products with legitimate uses that are abused by some people to get high ..., these products are made to get people high and marketed in illegitimate ways.

Dr. Roneet Lev, an emergency room physician and director of operations at Scripps Mercy Hospital, recently spoke at a press conference in San Diego addressing the problem of these products:

"Synthetic drugs and herbal drug products are not produced in a controlled laboratory environment," she explained. "Predicting the dangerous contaminants that could be inhaled when smoking Spice and other variations of synthetic marijuana is impossible. It's tragic to see young people admitted to hospital emergency rooms with heart problems and seizures caused by their ingestion of these drugs. As an emergency room physician, I'm gravely concerned about the potential harm these substances pose to residents, particularly our youth."

In addition to health concerns, these products have impacted public safety. On November 27, 2010, two masked men robbed the Spice Shack in Fallbrook of $1,400 worth of "herbal incense," less than a week after the DEA [Drug Enforcement Administration] announced the emergency scheduling of these products as a Schedule I [category given to drugs with high potential for abuse and no currently accepted medical use] Controlled Substance.

Easy Access, Availability, and Promotion of Synthetic Drugs

Like in many parts of the country, we have found Spice and similar products in liquor stores, cigarette stores, convenience stores, head shops, and newer specialty stores like Incense World in Oceanside and the Spice Shack in Fallbrook. During visits in November 2010 to a sample of approximately twelve such businesses in Oceanside and Vista, six were carrying synthetic marijuana. Unlike some products with legitimate uses that are abused by some people to get high (like Dust Off or solvents), these products are made to get people high and marketed in illegitimate ways. They come in multiple flavors such as watermelon, lemon-lime, blueberry, and mango and are labeled as incense. The liquor store in Vista where I recently purchased a sample of watermelon G.D.S. (GrandDaddySpice) displayed this "incense" in a locked case by the counter selling for $12 per 1.5 gram jar, while traditional incense sticks were on an open table selling for $1 for 10 sticks. Also in this case was "8 Ballz" bath salts selling for $25 for a small pouch. For anyone unfamiliar with the drug culture, an eight ball can refer to 1/8 ounce of drugs such as heroin, cocaine, or methamphetamine.

The product is labeled "not for human consumption" and sometimes includes a statement to "use only as directed," though no directions are included. We trained two of our high school youth coalition members to conduct purchase attempts at four stores in Vista, and the teens were only successful in purchasing the product at one store. The others required an I.D. to determine if they were over 18. While checking I.D. and refusing sales to minors is something our coalition actively promotes, in this case it further demonstrates that everyone knows these products are not incense, and that they *are* used for human consumption.

In the Mid-City area of San Diego, where colleagues of mine facilitate the Latino Youth Council, a youth advocate was outraged to find synthetic marijuana in foil packages resembling candy. "A friend of mine grabbed what he thought was a package of *Pop Rocks* off a store shelf. But then he noticed that it wasn't candy, it was fake pot, which we had learned about at a recent Latino Youth Council meeting. So he didn't buy it," shared Abigal Figueroa with the Latino Youth Council managed by Social Advocates for Youth (SAY) San Diego.

While retail outlets create a visible and convenient means for obtaining Spice, the internet is also a big supplier. As recently as March 27, 2011, [a website] purport[ed] to sell:

- *The only specialty incense products LEGAL EVERY-WHERE, including the military*

- *MORE effective than any previous generation K2 product! GUARANTEED TO SATISFY!*

- *WHOLESALE pricing available! Sell to anyone, anywhere, make MILLIONS like we have!*

Efforts Can Be Made to Combat the Problem

To address this blatant disregard for public health and safety by retail businesses, the Latino Youth Council recently launched the *Think Twice Before Selling Spice* campaign. As makers and distributors of these products are trying to stay one step ahead of the law by changing molecules or relabeling packages with statements such as "complies with emergency scheduling," teens are calling upon retailers to be responsible community partners.

They recently held a press conference in San Diego on March 4, 2011, in partnership with the DEA and launched a

Facebook page urging retailers to be responsible, and urging community members to refuse to shop at stores that continue to sell Spice.

"Protecting San Diegans from unregulated synthetic marijuana products is a quality-of-life issue that any retailer who is a member of our community should wholeheartedly support," said William Sherman, Acting Special Agent in Charge of the DEA's San Diego office. "The DEA calls on retailers to be part of the solution to limiting the reach of these dangerous substances."

As we learn the challenges and limitations in current regulations, we are prepared to advocate for additional tools to prevent the sale and distribution of these products in our communities.

Outreach, education, and training regarding synthetic marijuana products have occurred in many sectors throughout San Diego County. Throughout the Marine Corps, the issue was recently addressed by all prevention staff at a Directors meeting. Additional training has been provided to all personnel regarding the Marine Corps Code which states that *"possession, use, trafficking or distribution of any legal or illegal form of substance used with the intent of altering the human state of consciousness . . . is not tolerated . . . and will lead to administrative consequences."* Thus, the Marine Corp has been able to address the use of synthetic marijuana as a mind altering substance regardless of its legal classification, and several Marines have been separated from service because of using it. Classifying such products as Schedule I Controlled Substances will benefit by reducing their availability, particularly in retail stores.

In a similar manner, additional training and clarification has been issued through San Diego County Juvenile Probation and Drug Court Program. By court order, *"minor[s] shall not use or possess alcohol, a controlled substance, or any substance the minor knows or reasonably should know is a mind altering substance without a valid prescription and shall submit to testing for the detection of alcohol, controlled substances, or mind altering substances whenever directed by any law enforcement or Probation Officer."*

Elizabeth Urquhart, Director of Phoenix House San Diego, which provides adolescent residential and outpatient treatment services, shared that they have also addressed Spice and synthetic THC products during many staff training sessions. They also utilize drug-sniffing dogs at their residential facility that have been trained to detect Spice, along with other controlled substances.

Community education efforts have also been done at many levels, including informing parents and educators, law enforcement, teens, and political leaders at the local, state, and federal level. Our coalition has written news articles, met with local city officials and law enforcement representatives, met with local retail outlets, and presented at numerous community groups to increase awareness and understanding of the risks of synthetic drugs. As we learn the challenges and limitations in current regulations, we are prepared to advocate for additional tools to prevent the sale and distribution of these products in our communities.

It is critical to curtail the expanding marketing, availability, and use of synthetic marijuana.

How the Combating Dangerous Designer Drugs Act of 2011 Will Help Communities

The Combating Dangerous Designer Drugs Act of 2011 will take the source chemicals the DEA has identified within K2 and similar products and place them as Schedule I narcotics with other dangerous drugs.

The legislation will also amend the Controlled Substances Act, doubling the timeframe the Drug Enforcement Administration and the Department of Health and Human Services have to emergency schedule substances from 18 months to 36 months. This will allow for dangerous substances to be quickly removed from the market while being studied for permanent scheduling.

It is critical to curtail the expanding marketing, availability, and use of synthetic marijuana. We know the primary reasons people use Spice and similar products is for the legal cover it provides, as well as the likelihood of avoiding detection in drug tests. By classifying these products as Schedule I narcotics, communities can work with their local officials and law enforcement agencies to inform business owners and hold them accountable for following the law.

Why Community Coalitions Are Keys to Success

Community coalitions are an essential component in reducing emerging drug use trends such as K2 and Spice because they are already connected with the key sectors needed to take action, and understand that multiple strategies are necessary to reduce the availability and use of these products. Communities with existing anti-drug coalitions can identify and combat synthetic drug problems like K2 and Spice quickly and before they attain crisis proportions, and are ready to utilize important policy changes to improve conditions at the local level.

I've included a local example . . . to describe how our coalition partnered with the California Department of Alcoholic Beverage Control (ABC) in 2002 to specifically address the sale of drug paraphernalia in licensed alcohol establishments. Products in glass tubes, including air freshener, vitamin supplements, and plastic roses were commonly sold in liquor stores for $1 and were used as pipes to smoke meth and crack. Just as everyone knows Spice is smoked and not used as incense, everyone knew these were crack pipes and not decorative roses or air fresheners. In 2002, the California legislature amended language in the Business and Professions Code to more clearly define drug paraphernalia. Our coalition was able to partner with our local ABC office to send a letter to local retailers and follow up with personal visits to make sure they were in compliance. While we are not aware of any retailers facing actual penalties, the possibility of legal action was enough to reduce availability of these glass vial products from over 50% to less than 5% in retail outlets in our communities.

In a similar manner, local coalitions such as ours can utilize federal legislation such as this in our communities to dramatically reduce, if not eliminate, the availability of Spice and similar products. Synthetic drug use is a multi-dimensional problem that demands comprehensive, coordinated solutions involving the collaboration of multiple community sectors.

Organizations to Contact

The editors have compiled the following list of organizations concerned with the issues debated in this book. The descriptions are derived from materials provided by the organizations. All have publications or information available for interested readers. The list was compiled on the date of publication of the present volume; the information provided here may change. Be aware that many organizations take several weeks or longer to respond to inquiries, so allow as much time as possible.

American Council for Drug Education (ACDE)
164 W 74th St., New York, NY   10023
(800) 488-3784
e-mail: acde@phoenixhouse.org
website: www.acde.org

The American Council for Drug Education is a substance abuse prevention and education agency that develops programs and materials to inform the public about the harmful effects of abusing drugs and alcohol. In 1995, ACDE became an affiliate of Phoenix House, the largest private substance abuse treatment program in the United States. Among its publications are the "Got the Smarts?" knowledge quiz and fact sheets on various club drugs, including "Basic Facts about Drugs: GHB and Rohypnol" and "Basic Facts about Drugs: Ecstasy."

Canadian Centre on Substance Abuse (CCSA)
75 Albert St., Suite 500, Ottawa, ON   K1P 5E7
   Canada
(613) 235-4048 • fax: (613) 235-8101
e-mail: info@ccsa.ca
website: www.ccsa.ca

CCSA works to minimize the harm associated with the use of alcohol, tobacco, and other drugs by sponsoring public debates on this issue. It disseminates information on the nature, extent, and consequences of substance abuse and supports organizations involved in substance abuse treatment, prevention, and educational programming. It publishes the quarterly newsletter *Action News*, which is available on its website.

Canadian Foundation for Drug Policy (CFDP)

70 MacDonald St., Ottawa, ON   K2P 1H6
  Canada
(613) 236-1027 • fax: (613) 238-2891
e-mail: eoscapel@ca.inter.net
website: www.cfdp.ca

Founded by several of Canada's leading drug policy specialists, the Canadian Foundation for Drug Policy examines the objectives and consequences of Canada's drug laws and policies. When necessary, the foundation recommends alternatives that it believes would make Canada's drug policies more effective and humane. The CFDP discusses drug policy issues with the Canadian government, media, and general public. It also disseminates educational materials and maintains a "What's New" section on its website.

Cato Institute

1000 Massachusetts Ave. NW, Washington, DC   20001-5403
(202) 842-0200 • fax: (202) 842-3490
website: www.cato.org

The Cato Institute is a public policy research foundation dedicated to limiting the control of government and to protecting individual liberty. Cato, which strongly favors drug legalization, publishes the *Cato Journal* three times a year, the *Cato Policy Report* bimonthly, and the *Cato Papers on Public Policy*, all of which are available on its website.

Center for Cognitive Liberty & Ethics (CCLE)

PO Box 73481, Davis, CA   95617-3481
fax: (205) 449-3119
website: www.cognitiveliberty.org

The Center for Cognitive Liberty & Ethics is a nonprofit organization dedicated to protecting and advancing freedom of thought in the area of neurotechnologies. CCLE works to ensure that the application and regulation of new psychotropic drugs and neurotechnologies proceed with as few restrictions as possible and in a manner consistent with the fundamental right to freedom of thought. CCLE publishes the newsletter *Mind Matter*, the *Journal of Cognitive Liberties, CCLE Reports*, and various flyers and pamphlets, which can be found on the organization's website.

DanceSafe

527 28th Ave., Seattle, WA   98122
(888) 636-2411
e-mail: dsusa@dancesafe.org
website: www.dancesafe.org

DanceSafe is a nonprofit harm-reduction organization promoting health and safety within the rave and club communities. It provides information on drugs, safe sex, and other health issues and offers pill testing and adulterant screening. DanceSafe maintains a blog, website, and an online bookstore.

Drug Enforcement Administration (DEA)

Mailstop AES, 8701 Morrissette Dr., Springfield, VA   22152
(202) 307-1000
website: www.justice.gov/dea

The DEA is the federal agency charged with enforcing the nation's drug laws. The agency concentrates on stopping the smuggling and distribution of narcotics in the United States and abroad. It publishes the biweekly electronic newsletter *Dateline DEA*, the *DEA Drug Fact Sheets*, and the *Get Smart About Drugs* resource for parents, which includes "Drugs of Abuse" and "Prescription for Disaster: How Teens Abuse Medicine." These and other resources can be found on the agency's website.

Drug Policy Alliance

131 W 33rd St., 15th Floor, New York, NY   10001
(212) 613-8020 • fax: (212) 613-8021

e-mail: nyc@drugpolicy.org
website: www.drugpolicy.org

The Drug Policy Alliance is working to broaden the public debate on drug policy and to promote alternatives to the war on drugs based on science, compassion, health, and human rights. The organization promotes harm reduction, an alternative approach to drug policy and treatment that focuses on minimizing the adverse effects of both drug use and drug prohibition. The group publishes the newsletter *The Ally* and the booklet *Safety First: A Reality-Based Approach to Teens and Drugs*, as well as research briefs, fact sheets, and articles, all of which are available on its website.

Institute for Social Research (ISR)

The University of Michigan, PO Box 1248
Ann Arbor, MI   48106-1248
(734) 764-8354 • fax: (734) 647-4575
e-mail: isr-info@isr.umich.edu
website: www.isr.umich.edu

The Institute for Social Research at the University of Michigan, through its Survey Research Center, conducts the annual "Monitoring the Future" survey, which gathers data on drug use—including club drug use—and attitudes toward drugs among eighth-, tenth-, and twelfth-grade students. Survey results are published by the National Institute on Drug Abuse and are available on ISR's website.

Libertarian Party

2600 Virginia Ave. NW, Suite 200, Washington, DC   20037
(800) 353-2887
e-mail: info@lp.org
website: www.lp.org

The Libertarian Party is a political party whose goal is to protect individual rights and liberties. It advocates the repeal of all laws prohibiting the production, sale, possession, or use of drugs. The party believes law enforcement should focus on preventing violent crimes against persons and property rather than on prosecuting people who use drugs. Its website includes the bimonthly *Libertarian Party News* and periodic *Issues Papers* and distributes a compilation of articles supporting drug legalization.

Multidisciplinary Association for Psychedelic Studies (MAPS)

1215 Mission St., Santa Cruz, CA   95060-9989
(831) 429-6362 • fax: (831) 429-6370
e-mail: askmaps@maps.org
website: www.maps.org

The Multidisciplinary Association for Psychedelic Studies is a nonprofit research and educational organization that assists scientists to design, fund, obtain approval for, and report on studies into the risks and benefits of MDMA (Ecstasy), psychedelic drugs, and marijuana. MAPS seeks to end the fear that surrounds psychedelic and marijuana research. The organization publishes an e-mail newsletter, the *MAPS Bulletin*, and various research papers, and it maintains an online book store.

National Center on Addiction and Substance Abuse (CASA)

633 3rd Ave., 19th Floor, New York, NY   10017-6706
(212) 841-5200
website: www.casacolumbia.org

The National Center on Addiction and Substance Abuse at Columbia University is a private, nonprofit organization that works to educate the public about the hazards of chemical dependency. The organization supports treatment as the best way to reduce chemical dependency. It produces publications describing the harmful effects of alcohol and drug addiction and effective ways to address the problem of substance abuse. Many reports, and the *Casa Inside* newsletter, are available at the organization's website.

National Institute on Drug Abuse (NIDA)
6001 Executive Blvd., Room 5213, MSC 9561
Bethesda, MD   20892-9561
(301) 443-1124
e-mail: information@nida.nih.gov
website: www.drugabuse.gov

NIDA supports and conducts research on drug abuse—including the yearly "Monitoring the Future" survey—in order to improve addiction prevention, treatment, and policy efforts. It publishes the monthly *NIDA Notes* online newsletter; the periodic *Drug Facts*, which includes "Spice" (synthetic marijuana); and a catalog of research reports and public education materials such as *Drugs, Brains, and Behavior—The Science of Addiction.*

Office of National Drug Control Policy (ONDCP)
Executive Office of the President
Drugs and Crime Clearinghouse, Rockville, MD   20849-6000
(800) 666-3332 • fax: (301) 519-5212
website: www.whitehouse.gov/ondcp

The Office of National Drug Control Policy is responsible for formulating the government's national drug strategy and the president's antidrug policy, as well as coordinating the federal agencies responsible for stopping drug trafficking. This effort includes an emphasis on community-based prevention programs, early intervention programs in health-care settings, and funding for scientific research on drug use. ONDCP maintains a blog on its website and provides drug policy studies upon request.

RAND Corporation
1700 Main St., Santa Monica, CA   90407-2138
(310) 393-0411
website: www.rand.org

The RAND Corporation is a research institution that seeks to improve public policy through research and analysis. Rand's Drug Policy Research Center publishes information on the costs, prevention, and treatment of alcohol and drug abuse as well as on trends in drug law enforcement. Among its drug policy and trends reports are "Marijuana Legalization" and "Assessing Drug Control Priorities in the Federal Budget," and the research brief "Better Understanding Efforts to Reduce the Supply of Illicit Drugs."

Reason Foundation

3415 S Sepulveda Blvd., Suite 400, Los Angeles, CA   90034
(310) 391-2245 • fax: (310) 391-4395
website: www.reason.org

Founded in 1978, the Reason Foundation is a nonprofit public policy organization that researches contemporary social and political problems and promotes a libertarian philosophy and free-market principles. It publishes the monthly *Reason* magazine, which contains articles and editorials critical of the war on drugs and smoking regulation.

Bibliography

Books

Waln K. Brown and J. Frederick Garman
Hallucinogenic Drugs (Parent Guides to Childhood Drug Use), 3rd ed. Tallahassee, FL: William Gladden Foundation Press, 2011.

Gary Paul Byrne
The Drug Attraction: What Parents Need to Know to Keep Kids Out of Trouble. Seattle, WA: CreateSpace, 2011.

Enno Freye and Joseph V. Levy
Pharmacology and Abuse of Cocaine, Amphetamines, Ecstasy and Related Designer Drugs. New York: Springer, 2009.

Glen R. Hanson, Peter J. Venturelli, and Annette E. Fleckenstein
Drugs and Society. Burlington, MA: Jones & Bartlett Learning, 2012.

Darryl S. Inaba, William E. Cohen, Elizabeth von Radics, and Ellen K. Cholewa
Uppers, Downers, All Arounders: Physical and Mental Effects of Psychoactive Drugs, 7th ed. Ashland, OR: CNS Publications, 2011.

Cynthia Kuhn, Scott Swartzwelder, and Wilkie Wilson
Buzzed: The Straight Facts About the Most Used and Abused Drugs from Alcohol to Ecstasy. New York: W.W. Norton, 2008.

Sandra Augustyn
Lawton, ed.

Drug Information for Teens: Health Tips About the Physical and Mental Effects of Substance Abuse, 2nd ed. Detroit, MI: Omnigraphics, 2006.

Harvey Milkman
and Stanley
Sunderwirth

Craving for Ecstasy and Natural Highs: A Positive Approach to Mood Alteration. Thousand Oaks, CA: Sage Publications, 2010.

Edgar-Andre
Montigny

The Real Dope: Social, Legal, and Historical Perspectives on the Regulation of Drugs in Canada. Toronto, Canada: University of Toronto Press, 2011.

Jorg Ornoy and
Xiaoling He, eds.

Methamphetamines: Abuse, Health Effects and Treatment Options. Hauppauge, NY: Nova Science Publishers, 2012.

David Parnell and
Amy Hammond
Hagberg

Facing the Dragon: How a Desperate Act Pulled One Addict Out of Methamphetamine Hell. Deerfield Beach, FL: Health Communications, Inc., 2010.

Simon Reynolds

Energy Flash: A Journey Through Rave Music and Dance Culture. Berkeley, CA: Soft Skull Press, 2012.

Marguerite
Rodger

Party and Club Drugs. New York: Crabtree Publishing Company, 2011.

Bill Sanders

Drugs, Clubs and Young People: Sociological and Public Health Perspectives. Farnham, Surrey, United Kingdom: Ashgate Publishing, 2006.

Nic Sheff

Tweak: Growing Up on Methamphetamines. New York: Atheneum Books for Young Readers, 2009.

Steve Sussman and Susan L. Ames

Drug Abuse: Concepts, Prevention, and Cessation. Cambridge, MA: Cambridge University Press, 2008.

Arnold M. Washton and Joan Ellen Zweben

Cocaine & Methamphetamine Addiction: Treatment, Recovery, and Relapse Prevention. New York: W.W. Norton, 2008.

Arlene N. Weisz and Beverly M. Black

Programs to Reduce Teen Dating Violence and Sexual Assault: Perspectives on What Works. New York: Columbia University Press, 2009.

Periodicals and Internet Sources

Richard Alleyne

"Ketamine Is 'Magic Drug' for Depression," *The Telegraph*, August 19, 2010.

Brent Begin

"Drug Overdoses Spur Effort to Outlaw Raves," *San Francisco Examiner*, December 22, 2010.

Madonna Behen

"Researchers Use Ecstasy to Treat PTSD," *Business Week*, July 19, 2010.

Evelyn Block

"Teens and Parents Need to Be Aware of the Dangers of Club Drugs," Examiner.com, October 27, 2009. www.examiner.com.

Bruce Bower	"Club Drug Tied to Out-of-Body Sensations," *Science News*, March 26, 2011.
Becky Campbell	"Fake Drugs, Real Consequences," *Johnson City Press*, February 5, 2012.
Denis Campbell	"Scientists Study Possible Health Benefits of LSD and Ecstasy," *The Guardian*, October 23, 2009.
Matthew Cardinale	"US House Bans Synthetic Marijuana After Heated Debate," Atlanta Progressive News, December 15, 2011. www.atlantaprogressivenews.com.
Nick Carraway	"The Addictive Yet Deadly Spice (Military Deal with New Drugs)," Free Republic, November 25, 2011. www.freerepublic.com.
John Cloud	"Ecstasy Shows Promise in Relieving PTSD," *Time*, July 10, 2010.
John Cloud	"Is Ketamine a Quick Fix for Hard-to-Treat Depression?" *Time*, August 2, 2010.
Jamie Doward	"Ecstasy Is Back in Clubs as Newly Potent Drug Is Taken with 'Legal Highs'," *The Observer*, November 19, 2011.
European Monitoring Centre for Drugs and Drug Addiction	"Understanding the 'Spice' Phenomenon," *EMCDDA Thematic Papers*, November 2009.

Howard Frank — "Popular Club Drug Replaced by a More Toxic One: Cloud Nine," *Pocono Record*, January 18, 2012.

Carrie Gann — "Caffeine Mist Is a 'Club Drug,' Says Schumer," ABCNews.com, December 23, 2011. www.abcnews.com.

Abby Goodnough and Katie Zezima — "An Alarming New Stimulant, Legal in Many States," *New York Times*, July 16, 2011.

Joe Gould — "Legal High Becomes 'Horrible Dream,'" *Military Times*, October 2, 2010. www.militarytimes.com.

Joe Gould — "Army Targets Designer Drugs, Bans Spice," *Army Times*, August 27, 2011.

Elizabeth Hartney — "Designer Drugs: Club Drugs Don't Deliver on Promise," About.com, updated June 23, 2011. www.about.com.

Allan Laing — "Trials Show Ecstasy Helps Post-Traumatic Stress Disorder," *Caledonian Mercury*, April 19, 2010.

Donna Leinwand — "Survey: More Teens Using Synthetic Drugs," *USA Today*, December 24, 2011.

Robin McKie — "Ecstasy Does Not Wreck the Mind, Study Claims," *The Guardian*, February 19, 2011.

National Association of Boards of Pharmacy	"Federal and State Governments Take Action to Stem Onslaught of Two New Classes of Synthetic Drugs," *NABP Newsletter*, February 2012.
National Institutes of Health	"InfoFacts: Methamphetamine," National Institute on Drug Abuse, March 2010. www.drugabuse.gov.
Christian Nordquist	"Modified Ecstasy Compounds Have Powerful Anti-Cancer Properties," *Medical News Today*, August 21, 2011.
Brandice J. O'Brien	"Investigation Nabs 30 Air Force Spice Users," US Air Force, June 14, 2011. www.af.mil.
Sarah Payne	"Effects of Bath Salts Comparable to Drugs Such as LSD, Ecstasy, PCP," *Daily Free Press*, February 22, 2011.
Max Pemberton	"I Took Mephedrone and I Liked It," *The Telegraph*, March 20, 2010.
Pauline Repard	"End to Sales of Synthetic Drugs Urged: Authorities Warn Retailers that Dangerous 'Spice,' 'Bath Salts' Must Come Off Shelves," *San Diego Union Tribune*, February 1, 2012.
Simon Reynolds	"Feeling Wonky: Is It Ketamine's Turn to Drive Club Culture?" *The Guardian*, March 5, 2009.
Maia Szalavitz	"Ecstasy as Therapy: Have Some of Its Negative Effects Been Overblown?" *Time*, February 18, 2011.

Maia Szalavitz	"A Mystery Partly Solved: How the 'Club Drug' Ketamine Lifts Depression So Quickly," *Time*, June 15, 2011.
Jeanne Whalen	"In Quest for 'Legal High,' Chemists Outfox Law," *Wall Street Journal*, October 29, 2010.
Sarah C.P. Williams	"Why Ketamine Makes You Happy," *Science NOW*, June 15, 2011.
Jessica Winter	"Can a Single Pill Change Your Life?" *Oprah Magazine*, February 2011.
Sam Wolfson	"Mephedrone—How Dangerous Is the UK's Favourite New Drug?" *NME*, February 8, 2010. www.nme.com.

Index